EDITORIAL

This issue is the culmination of work across the profession and academia, under the leadership of our Special Issue Guest Editors Dr Mike Jones and Rachel Tropea. Mike and Rachel have worked with authors to produce this special issue over the past 18 months, and the outcome is a collection of papers, reflections and a significant conversation that document the current state of the 'two sides of the same coin' in archival research and practice, and looks to the future.

Special issues of *Archives and Manuscripts* play an important role in creating spaces for focussed discussion on contemporary topics, and for documenting the key issues for the society and profession at a moment in time. Past special issues reflect this temporality – in 2019 the special issue 'After the Digital Revolution' considered the challenges of the digital in literary archives, whereas 25 years earlier the journal published a special issue that considered the broader challenge of 'Electronic recordkeeping: Issues and perspectives' (1994). The nuanced focus in 2019 on digital literary archives was enabled by the previous decades worth of research and publishing in the field.

We are excited to have more special issues on the horizon, including a 2025 issue planned to document the outcomes of the *Tandanya-Adelaide Declaration Symposium*, held in Christchurch, Aotearoa in October 2024. We encourage academics and professionals to consider *Archives and Manuscripts* as a potential home for collaborative ideas and engagement through special issue proposals.

Angela Schilling
Dr Jessie Lymn
General Editors

INTRODUCTION

Two Sides of the Same Coin? Exploring the Relationship Between Archival Research and Practice

Mike Jones[1]* and Rachel Tropea[2]

[1]University of Tasmania; [2]RMIT University

In 2009, a group of archivists, data archivists, and academics converged on a cottage at the edge of the Australian National University (ANU) campus carrying digital cameras, archive boxes, markers, labels, and laptops. Spread over several rooms were cardboard boxes of all shapes and sizes, some collapsing under the weight of their contents, along with shelves of ring binders, continuous form paper printouts, stacks of photocopies, piles of loose records, publications, large format handwritten data tables, and more – the accumulated papers of researchers Len Smith and Gordon Briscoe.

For several days the cottage was filled with conversations that spilled out into lunch breaks, dinners, and drinks at the ANU bar. Some were about archival principles, accession processes, capturing and preserving data on computer punch cards, options for digitising large format data sheets, and how to develop a series structure. Others covered the history of census data, demography, prosopography, and early social science computing; how to generate Aboriginal population estimates; Gordon Briscoe's experiences as one of the first Aboriginal people to obtain a PhD at an Australian University; and the policing of Aboriginal and Torres Strait Islander communities in the early twentieth century. At the same time the archivists introduced their colleagues to key archival concepts and led a process of labelling boxes, surveying and documenting the order of the records as found, boxing up loose material, considering provenance, and capturing accession metadata in the standards-based Heritage Documentation Management System (HDMS). It was a fascinating few days, filled with research, theoretical debate, and the time-bound practicalities of tackling a large unlisted archive. As Michelle Caswell writes:

> One of the things I love about archival studies is that, on the one hand, you can discuss really abstract theoretical concepts but at the end of the day, you have to do something as an archivist ... do I keep this particular record or not? Do I digitize it? What words do I use to describe it? The rubber meets the road.[1]

Work on Smith and Briscoe's articles – collectively named *Documenting Demography and Health Records of Aboriginal and Torres Strait Islanders* – continues to this day, the complex archive raising issues related to digitisation and digital preservation, data archiving, Indigenous data sovereignty, privacy, and ethics that remain the subject of ongoing research and practice.

---

*Correspondence: Mike Jones, Email: info@mikejonesonline.com

Among the archivists working in the ANU cottage were the authors and guest editors of this issue of *Archives & Manuscripts*, Mike Jones and Rachel Tropea. We started working together in 2008 at the University of Melbourne's eScholarship Research Centre (ESRC)[2] under the leadership of Gavan McCarthy and Joanne Evans. It was here our long-standing interest in the intersections between theory, research and practice in archives began. Like many staff at the ESRC we worked across boundaries: as archivists without a repository, working for a range of large and small institutions; based in the library while collaborating with multiple university faculties; employed as professional staff while working on academic research projects and producing traditional and non-traditional research outputs; and exploring theoretical ideas while remaining engaged in numerous projects that allowed us to (in McCarthy's words) 'get our hands dirty'. Our collaborators were archivists, librarians, developers, information technology staff, academics, public servants, community members, and activists. The team implemented early incarnations of ISAD(G), EAD, ISAAR(CPF) and EAC through the HDMS and Online Heritage Resource Manager (OHRM) and went to work with these tools archiving Victoria's State Electricity Commission, documenting the history of Australian Science, and capturing the stories of Australian women, among many other projects.[3] We also worked with communities on restorative justice projects such as *Find & Connect* and *Return, Reconcile, Renew*,[4] using participatory and action research methods.

In many ways the ESRC was unique. There were no other places in Australia where we could perform work like this, and the Centre's longevity was dependent on continuing support from people within an organisation often poorly suited to groups that did not fit neatly within existing frameworks of academic research or service provision. Heather MacNeil writes:

> whether theory is actualized in practice will depend less on the power of the theory than on the actions of individuals, professional organizations, and institutions. We may not control institutional resources and priorities to the extent we would like … We do, however, have control over the direction in which we move as individuals and as a profession.[5]

When institutional priorities shifted and the Centre closed in 2020, Mike moved into academia and Rachel into a managerial role at a university archive. Keeping a foot in both worlds, or working in the in between, is now harder, but we have both tried in our own ways to retain control over the directions we move in, and remain committed to working with the broader profession. In 2018 Rachel and her colleagues at University of Melbourne started a Critical Archives Reading Group[6] for memory workers interested in the nexus between academic and practitioner work in archives, and how they influence or could influence each other. The readings are framed within postcolonialism, critical race studies, feminism, queer theory and deconstructionism, and themes of social justice and equity.[7] After completing his PhD, Mike moved into roles in academic history departments while continuing to regularly write and speak about archives and the GLAM sector. Pursuing cross-disciplinary work in history, museums, archives, and Indigenous studies, he continues to seek out opportunities that allow him to 'get his hands dirty'.

Mike is also an active member of the Australian Society of Archivists (ASA), and is the inaugural convenor of the Research and Education Special Interest Group (REDSIG) from which the idea for this issue emerged. The objectives of REDSIG include: to develop Australia's research capacity and capability with regard to archives; to promote research capability as a valued professional attribute for all archivists and affiliated professionals, and foster opportunities, which create and invigorate connections between archival theory and practice in Australia and to raise awareness of and advocate for the value of archival scholarship, thinking, and practice.[8]

The process of putting together this special issue on research and practice has been fascinating. We are very grateful to all of the contributors who made time among the seemingly endless stream of online meetings, competing deadlines (including impending PhD submission dates!) and busy lives to reflect on these ideas and communicate their thoughts to the broader community. This willingness to engage helps to ensure that archival work continues to adapt and remain relevant in a rapidly changing world.

Which is not to say these preoccupations are new. Our call for papers for this issue included a quote from Benjamin Brewster, writing in 1882: 'In theory, there is no difference between theory and practice, while in practice there is'.[9]

In the first half of the twentieth century archivists did little to separate the two. Often the terms were combined to reference the guiding principles (provenance, original order, *respect des fonds*) and core activities (appraisal, arrangement, description, preservation, provision of access) that characterise archival work. For example, the *Manual for the Arrangement and Description of Archives* (1898) has been called the 'starting point of archival theory and methodology'[10]; and Hilary Jenkinson's 1922 *A Manual of Archive Administration* sought to draw together 'a complete body of illustration of general Archive theory and practice' based on English archives.[11] In North America Solon J. Buck (Second Archivist of the United States) used the phrase 'principles and techniques' to mean something similar,[12] as did Theodore R. Schellenberg whose *The Management of Archives* was divided into two parts: 'Development of Principles and Techniques,' and 'Application of Principles and Techniques'.

Perhaps in part due to such language, by the early 1980s Harold Pinkett argued that a distinct American archival *theory* did not exist. Archives, according to Pinkett, combined European principles with 'pragmatic concepts'.[13] Such claims were part of an emerging debate in North America that would run for the next 20 years. Frank Burke was among the first, suggesting archives had policies and procedures rather than 'theories'. While some archivists might consider moving to the academy to ponder research questions such as the social context of records creation, the nature of history, and the purpose of archivists, Burke did not see these as part of day-to-day work: 'It is reasonable to expect that on slow days and after hours, when one's spouse is otherwise occupied, the kids are in bed, and the income tax is finished, a few archivists will contemplate these mysteries'.[14]

John W. Roberts went further in two strident articles for *American Archivist*: 'Archival Theory: Much Ado about Shelving' (1987), and 'Archival Theory: Myth or Banality?' (1990). The first piece pulls few punches, suggesting archival theory arises not from an objective need, but 'from an emotional need for greater professional acceptance'.[15] He claims concepts such as provenance and original order as 'largely practical tools,' critiques theorists for stating the obvious 'in unduly complicated terms,' and argues that many of the theoretical questions proposed by people such as Burke are not in fact archival questions. In fact, they provide 'no assistance whatsoever' in carrying out what is at its heart 'a fairly straight-forward, down to earth service occupation'.[16] He concludes:

> Great things are happening in the world of ideas. Poems are being written, symphonies composed, diseases mastered, historical eras probed, and economic dilemmas analyzed. In the midst of all this, it is extreme intellectual silliness to boggle oneself with such preposterous phantoms as archival paradigms, symbiotic links of medium and message, philosophy of mylar, and other prostheses that some archivists would thrust forward as credentials to sit at the grown-ups' table.[17]

His second article goes even further, suggesting the whole of archival work 'can be known empirically,' criticising theoretical research for uncovering 'vacuous principles,' and dismissing archival theory as unimportant, intellectually frivolous, narcissistic, self-involved, and 'an outgrowth of the archival profession's colossal inferiority complex'.[18]

Many questioned Roberts' position. Some did so in *American Archivist*, including amused Norwegian archivist Ole Kolsrud: 'How seriously is Roberts to be taken? He is not the first barbarian I have come across among archivists, but at least he is an entertaining one'.[19] But the most effective responses were published across the border, in the Canadian journal *Archivaria*. The 1990s saw, among others: Mary Sue Stephenson, on the close and productive relationships between theorists, writers, researchers, and practitioners in archives (unlike in library science) and the dangers of trying to build a wall between research and practice; Terry Eastwood, who responded to Roberts with a clear outline of the importance of theory, its object, and its relation to method and practice; Heather MacNeil on the foundational role of theory and methodological principles in archival work; and Preben Mortensen, who concludes that, despite the views of Roberts and other 'anti-theoretical' archivists, theory and practice are in fact inseparable.[20]

Meanwhile, in the second half of the twentieth century Australia started to develop its own ways of working. In his foreword to Schellenberg's *Modern Archives*, the Commonwealth National Librarian and Archival Authority, H.L. White, recognised that the English and European focus on earlier records was inhibiting 'the necessary thinking and experiment which the control of modern records in young countries requires. Despite this, there is evidence that some of the younger countries are in fact breaking new ground'.[21] We see this in the work of Commonwealth Archivist Ian Maclean and colleagues. While they initially drew on Jenkinson (who started out working on medieval records) and Schellenberg (who visited as an adviser in 1954[22]), their attempts to use the 'record group' concept to arrange and describe Australian Government records were fraught, in part due to the rate of change in Government departments and bureaucracy in the twentieth century. New ground was then broken in the 1960s, with the well-documented development of the Australian series system by Peter J. Scott.[23]

The series system was more than just a practical solution to a practical problem. As Barbara Reed has argued, Scott was a conceptual thinker who 'consciously pursued archival theory' to produce a framework for practice that influenced recordkeeping and continuum theorists, archival standards development, digital records management, and more.[24] While continuum theory in particular is often held up as complex and difficult (as discussed in the conversation piece included in this issue), these practical roots and its role as a framework for action mean that many in the community were keen to apply the continuum in their work. Sue McKemmish writes of the community of practice that emerged in Australia during the 1990s, 'made up of records managers and archivists, consultants, educators and researchers, archival institutions, corporate records and archives programs, and professional associations, who consciously worked within an evolving records continuum framework, and adopted post-custodial approaches to recordkeeping and archiving'.[25]

Though McKemmish (like her predecessors) repeatedly uses the phrase 'theory and practice,' and references archival theorists, it is notable that her description of the community of practice does not explicitly include theory or theorists. Instead McKemmish refers to researchers more broadly, elsewhere highlighting how the continuum – including continuum theory, the continuum framework, the continuum model, and 'continuum thinking and practice' – is itself 'a distillation of research findings drawn from discourse, literary warrant and historical analysis, as well as case studies, participant observation and reflection'.[26]

As touched on by James Lowry and Elliot Freeman in this issue, research and theory are not necessarily the same thing, and their relationship to practice can vary. Lowry notes that some researchers do significant translation work themselves, examining how theories from disparate fields can be applied in practice, while in other cases (like some continuum theory work) this translation work mostly happens outside of the research space, including through communities of practice like those described by McKemmish.

However, given the tendency to conflate research and theory (noticed by Freeman, and evident in our call for papers for this issue), perhaps our conversation piece should have started with the basics: what is archival research, and (just as importantly) *where* is archival research? Carol Couture and Daniel Ducharme provided a useful summary in 2005, developing a typology of research fields in archival science, including the role of archives in society; the management of archival programmes; investigations into different types of records (including digital and other media); and archival ethics.[27] Research happens in universities and educational institutions; but professionals in a range of institutions also ask research questions and use research methodologies in their work, as do consultants, and project teams initiated by sectoral organisations such as the ASA, Records and Information Management Practitioners Alliance (RIMPA), GLAM Peak, and the International Council on Archives (ICA). As Luciana Duranti and Givanni Michetti note, some of this research focus on ideas and activities that are clearly part of the 'archival field' (investigating the nature of records, key principles like original order, or exploring provenance), while other research brings in theories, concepts, and methodologies from elsewhere to help understand archives and records, and to develop (or seek to change) professional practice.[28] External influences include closely allied disciplines such as history, knowledge management, computer science, and library science, as well as diverse theoretical and methodological approaches drawn from feminist theory, Critical Race Theory, Indigenous standpoint theory, data sovereignty, postcolonial studies, queer theory, and so on.[29]

Most of this work is pursued with at least one eye on practice. Archival science has long been recognised as an applied science, combining diverse theories and methodologies with empirical evidence and experience, developed and tested through practice.[30] Michelle Caswell writes: 'For most archival studies scholars, our research is rooted in practice. Most of us either worked as archivists before becoming researchers or still have a significant practice on the side … my research informs my practice and my practice informs my research'.[31] Theoretical discussions and in-depth research can be fascinating in their own right, but if they do not achieve anything useful in the world perhaps (as suggested by Burke) we should leave them to those times out of hours when partners are occupied, kids are in bed, and our taxes are done. When combined with practice though, such discussions are a vital part of ensuring our profession remains relevant and responsive. Schellenberg argues that even supposedly foundational principles such as provenance and original order 'should be applied only insofar as something can be achieved by their application'.[32]

Archival research is about continuing to ask such questions. What should we aim to achieve by the application of principles, theories and methods in the archival field? How can we best achieve these things? What are the current limitations of practice? How can we continue to do things better? How do we make ourselves accountable for our actions along the way? As Kieran Hegarty and Jodie Boyd note in the introduction to the recent 'research and practice' issue of the *Journal of Critical Library and Information Studies*, we cannot effectively answer these questions by dividing research and practice; nor do we gain by trying to unite the two. Instead we need to embrace multiplicity, recognising diverse perspectives and ways of working and the many positions and relationships we as individuals can and do hold within the archival field.[33]

In keeping with this, the contributors to this special issue of *Archives & Manuscripts* speak from multiple perspectives. In the opening Conversation piece, eight 'academics' and 'practitioners' (Mike Jones and Rachel Tropea with Rose Barrowcliffe, Annie Cameron,

Elliot Freeman, James Lowry, Duncan Loxton, and Eva Samaras) reflect on the arbitrary separation or conflation of research, theory and practice in archives. Participants discuss how archival education and theory is relevant to practice and practitioners and vice versa and the ways in which research can be theoretical, directed, applied, and practical. In doing so, the participants provide a contemporary perspective on many of the ideas summarised above.

Articles from Kirsten Thorpe; Frank Golding, Sue McKemmish and Barbara Reed; and Catherine Nicholls focus on the role of research in action, and how it can serve individuals and communities. Thorpe examines how practice and research methodologies aligned with Indigenous ways of knowing, being and doing – including Indigenous methodologies such as Yarning, Indigenous Standpoint and Indigenous Storywork – support First Nations archival priorities and increase Indigenous agency and well-being in the archives. In fact, Thorpe writes: 'An Indigenous-led and community-driven approach has the potential to bring mutual benefits for all involved'. Golding, McKemmish and Reed explore the challenges of actualising community-centred, participatory recordkeeping and archiving research in practice, using the implementation of the Charter of Lifelong Rights in Childhood Recordkeeping in Out of Home Care as an illustrative example. Catherine Nicholls discusses her research journey through autoethnographic narrative, providing insight into the various paths practitioners and researchers take through and between these domains. Research and professional development are rarely linear or neat, and research does not necessitate taking on a passive, formal, or supposedly 'objective' voice. As Nicholls shows, it can also be personal and reflective.

James Doig and Vanessa Finney reflect on the impact of archival thought in national events and institutions in recent history. Doig analyses the theoretical ideas developed by Terry Cook, Frank Upward and others in the 1990s, and explores the degree to which they have been implemented within foundational policy, recordkeeping standards and guidance in Australia. Focusing on the results of the National Archives *Big Data Project* (2022) he explores the enduring impact of these post-custodial concepts, including the development of the world-first records management standard *AS 4390 – 1996 Records Management* – work that involved close collaboration between researchers and practitioners who espoused post-custodial approaches to archival and records management. Finney reaches further back when discussing the archival turn in Australia's colonial-era museums and in particular Australia's first and oldest cultural-scientific institution, The Australian Museum (AM), founded in 1827. Citing examples of key initiatives such as 'cultural diplomacy' work around the Thomas Dick Birrpai Collection, Finney explores the significant act of re-making archival practice, reviewing past protocols, knowledge structures, and descriptive standards to reimagine 'museum-archival practice and the possibilities (and challenges) for opening the archives to new ways of encounter, reading and use'.

Our perception of the archives depends on whether we are staff, contractor, maintainer, manager, researcher, scholar, student, donor, subject of the records, or (as is often the case) a mixture of these roles. The issue concludes with two pieces that highlight the many different hats and life experiences we bring to our encounter with the archive. Master's student Bryony Cavallaro reflects on the interplay between her theoretical education, gamer experience and practicum at the Digital Heritage Lab in shaping her knowledge and skills as a digital archivist, while Jessica Moran shows how her experience as a manager and steward of archival collections and digitisation projects, work as a researcher and editor, and knowledge of archival theory have influenced her approach to digital preservation. Theory, research and practice are intertwined, allowing for a more nuanced, considered and multi-layered effort.

Throughout, a consistent theme emerges. Many in the archival field have moved beyond the debates of the twentieth century about the existence and relevance of theory, with recent generations of archivists less inclined than their predecessors to draw distinctions. While the mix may differ depending on context, research, theory, and practice are all part of what we do.

There are many developments that threaten our ability to work effectively in this way. As MacNeil notes, actualising theory in practice relies on individuals, professional organisations, and institutions working together. At a time when institutional and research funding cuts continue to bite, when universities are closing or downsizing archives and information studies courses across the country, when so many academics remain precariously employed, when governments and corporations pursue automation and poorly-implemented IT solutions, and when archivists and records managers are faced with growing backlogs and dwindling resources – when all this provides the context for our day-to-day work, deep engagement with research and theory might seem a luxury only accessible to a lucky few.

But we must use the control we have over our individual and professional pathways to continue to make space for this essential work. Acting collectively, we can advocate for the value of archival research and practice; remain engaged and involved in communities; foster relationships; actively think about what we do and why we do it; discuss archival ideas with each other, and with colleagues from other professions and disciplines; read and engage with new developments in theory and practice; ask for a seat at the table; listen and make space for other voices and perspectives; and keep asking questions.

Acknowledgements

Thank you to everyone who contributed to this issue, to our peer reviewers for your considered feedback, and to the general editors of *Archives & Manuscripts* for your support along the way.

We would like to acknowledge the *Journal of Critical Library and Information Studies*, a constant source of inspiration driving us to forge ahead with the important work of interrogating what it means to be an archivist[34]; to Kirsten Thorpe, whose work and article 'Transformative Praxis – Building Spaces for Indigenous Self-Determination in Libraries and Archives'[35] inspired Rachel to start the Critical Archives Reading Group; to all the members of the Research and Education Special Interest Group who have attended meetings and catchups, and contributed to the development of the SIG; and to all the archival researchers, theorists, and practitioners we have worked with over the years. Without the broader collective our work would not be what it is today.

Notes

1. Michelle Caswell and Rachel Tropea, 'Interview with Michelle Caswell,' Archive Matters, no. 116, May 5, 2021, n.p.
2. The eScholarship Research Centre (ESRC) (2007–2020) was previously known as the Australian Science and Technology Heritage Centre (Austehc) (1999–2006), and Australian Science Archives Project (ASAP) (1985–1989). For more information, see https://www.eoas.info/biogs/A002361b.htm.
3. 'About,' Encyclopedia of Australian Science and Innovation, https://www.eoas.info/about.html (accessed March 2024); 'About,' Australian Women's Register, https://www.womenaustralia.info/about/ (accessed 25 July 2024).
4. https://www.findandconnect.gov.au/ and https://returnreconcilerenew.info/
5. Heather MacNeil, 'Archival Theory and Practice: Between Two Paradigms,' Archivaria, February 6, 1994, 16.
6. https://www.criticalarchivesreading.com/
7. About – Critical Archives Reading Group, URL: https://www.criticalarchivesreading.com/p/about.html (accessed March 2024).
8. A full list of the REDSIG objectives are available in the REDSIG Rules, available here: https://www.archivists.org.au/community/research-and-education
9. Benjamin Brewster, *The Yale Literary Magazine*, February 1882, quoted in 'In Theory There Is No Difference Between Theory and Practice, While In Practice There Is,' Quote Investigator, April 14, 2018, https://quoteinvestigator.com/2018/04/14/theory/. Our call for papers featured an adapted version of this

quote: 'In theory, there is no difference between theory and practice. But, in practice, there is'. Variations on this phrase are often misattributed, including to Yogi Berra, Albert Einstein, Richard Feynman, and various computer scientists.
10. Peter Horsman, Eric Ketelaar, Theo Thomassen, 'Introduction to the 2003 Reissue,' in Samuel Muller, Robert Fruin, and Johan Adriaan Feith, Manual for the Arrangement and Description of Archives: Drawn up by Direction of the Netherlands Association of Archivists, Translation of the 2nd ed., Society of American Archivists, Chicago, IL, 2003, p. v, http://hdl.handle.net/2027/mdp.39015057022447.
11. Hilary Jenkinson, A Manual of Archive Administration Including the Problems of War Archives and Archive Making, The Clarendon Press, Oxford, 1922, p. 17, http://archive.org/details/manualofarchivea00jenkuoft.
12. Solon J. Buck quoted in Lester Cappon, 'What, Then, Is There To Theorize About?,' The American Archivist, vol. 45, no. 1, January 1, 1982, p. 24. https://doi.org/10.17723/aarc.45.1.q03v972668401056
13. Harold Pinkett, 'American Archival Theory: The State of the Art,' The American Archivist, vol. 44, no. 3, July 1, 1981, p. 222. https://doi.org/10.17723/aarc.44.3.n22253t6262t2101
14. Frank G. Burke, 'The Future Course of Archival Theory in the United States,' The American Archivist, vol. 44, no. 1, 1981, p. 44. https://doi.org/10.17723/aarc.44.1.4853801307551286
15. John W. Roberts, 'Archival Theory: Much Ado about Shelving,' The American Archivist, vol. 50, no. 1, 1987, p. 67.
16. Roberts, p. 68, 69, 74.
17. Roberts, p. 74.
18. John Roberts, 'Archival Theory: Myth or Banality?,' The American Archivist, vol. 53, no. 1, 1990, p. 111, 112, 115, 119, 120. https://doi.org/10.17723/aarc.53.1.a56364w710276424
19. Ole Kolsrud, 'The Evolution of Basic Appraisal Principles – Some Comparative Observations,' The American Archivist, vol. 55, no. 1, January 1, 1992, p. 36. https://doi.org/10.17723/aarc.55.1.v05w2kg671667v6h
20. Mary Sue Stephenson, 'Deciding Not to Build the Wall: Research and the Archival Profession,' Archivaria, vol. 32, Summer 1991, pp. 145–51; Terry Eastwood, 'What Is Archival Theory and Why Is It Important?,' Archivaria, February 6, 1994, pp. 122–30; MacNeil, 'Archival Theory and Practice'; Preben Mortensen, 'The Place of Theory in Archival Practice,' Archivaria, vol. 47, February 16, 1999, http://www.archivaria.ca/index.php/archivaria/article/view/12695.
21. See H.L. White, 'Foreword,' in Theodore R. Schellenberg (ed.), Modern Archives: Principles and Techniques, University of Chicago Press, Chicago, Il, 1956, p. vii.
22. See Michael Piggott, 'The Visit of Dr. T.R. Schellenberg to Australia 1954: A Study of Its Origins and Some Repercussions on Archival Development in Australia', Masters, Sydney, Australia, University of New South Wales, 1989.
23. Adrian Cunningham, Laura Millar, and Barbara Reed, 'Peter J. Scott and the Australian 'Series' System: Its Origins, Features, Rationale, Impact and Continuing Relevance', International Congress on Archives, Brisbane, Australia, 2012, http://ica2012.ica.org/files/pdf/Full%20papers%20upload/ica12Final00414.pdf; see also Clive Smith, 'The Australian Series System,' Archivaria, vol. 40, January 1, 1995, http://www.archivaria.ca/index.php/archivaria/article/view/12098; Australian Society of Archivists, Peter J. Scott, and Adrian Cunningham (eds.), The Arrangement and Description of Archives amid Administrative and Technological Change: Essays and Reflections by and about Peter J. Scott, Australian Society of Archivists, Brisbane, 2010.
24. Barbara Reed, "Standing on the Shoulders of Giants': The Legacy of Peter Scott's Archival Thinking,' in Cunningham, Millar, and Reed (eds.), Peter J. Scott and the Australian 'Series' System: Its Origins, Features, Rationale, Impact and Continuing Relevance.
25. Sue McKemmish, 'Placing Records Continuum Theory and Practice,' Archival Science, vol. 1, no. 4, December 1, 2001, p. 336. https://doi.org/10.1007/BF02438901
26. McKemmish, p. 333.
27. Carol Couture and Daniel Ducharme, 'Research in Archival Science: A Status Report,' Archivaria, 2005, pp. 63–4.
28. Luciana Duranti and Giovanni Michetti, 'The Archival Method,' in Anne J. Gilliland, Sue McKemmish, and Andrew J. Lau (eds.), Research in the Archival Multiverse, Monash University Publishing, Clayton, Victoria, 2017, p. 80, http://www.oapen.org/search?identifier=628143.
29. For example, see Catherine Banks, 'The Influence of Feminist Archival Theory on State Archival Exhibitions,' Archives & Manuscripts, February 14, 2024, p. e10933. https://doi.org/10.37683/asa.v51.10933; Anthony W. Dunbar, 'Introducing Critical Race Theory to Archival Discourse: Getting the Conversation Started,' Archival Science, vol. 6, no. 1, March 1, 2006, pp. 109–29. https://doi.org/10.1007/s10502-006-9022-6;

Kirsten Thorpe, 'Unclasping the White Hand: Reclaiming and Refiguring the Archives to Support Indigenous Wellbeing and Sovereignty', PhD, Melbourne, Australia, Monash University, 2021.
30. Buck, quoted in Cappon, 'What, Then, Is There To Theorize About?,' p. 24.
31. Caswell and Tropea, 'Interview with Michelle Caswell'.
32. T. Schellenberg, 'Archival Principles of Arrangement,' The American Archivist, vol. 24, no. 1, January 1, 1961, p. 13. https://doi.org/10.17723/aarc.24.1.l330351406231083
33. Kieran Hegarty and Jodie Boyd, 'Useful Divides: Games of Truth in Library and Information Studies Research and Practice,' *Journal of Critical Library and Information Studies*, vol. 4, December 15, 2023, p. 21.
34. The Journal of Critical Library and Information Studies (JCLIS) is an online journal which 'aims to showcase innovative research that queries and critiques current and prevailing paradigms in library and information studies, in theory and practice through critical approaches and perspectives that originate from across the humanities and social science..' The issue: Vol. 4: Assemblage, Inquiry, and Common Work in Library and Information Studies is particularly relevant to our theme.
35. Kirsten Thorpe, 'Transformative Praxis – Building Spaces for Indigenous Self-Determination in Libraries and Archives,' 23 January 2019, *In the Library with the Lead Pipe*, URL: https://www.inthelibrarywiththeleadpipe.org/2019/transformative-praxis/.

IN CONVERSATION

Research and Practice – A Conversation

Mike Jones[1]*, Rachel Tropea[2], Rose Barrowcliffe[3], Annie Cameron[4], Elliot Freeman[5], James Lowry[6], Duncan Loxton[7] and Eva Samaras[8]

[1]University of Tasmania, [2]RMIT University, [3]Macquarie University, [4]Wangka Maya Pilbara Aboriginal Language Centre, [5]La Trobe University, [6]City University of New York, [7]University of Technology Sydney, [8]University of Melbourne

Introduction

Since the mid-20th century, Australia has gained recognition for its innovative approaches to archival practice and theory, including the Australian Series System and the Records Continuum Model. However, the relationship between archival work, records management, and contemporary theory and research is not always clear and can present challenges.

Mike Jones and Rachel Tropea invited a group of colleagues to explore these ideas in a recorded Zoom conversation on Monday, January 22, 2024. The participants then edited the transcript for clarity.

The conversation features the following participants, in order of speaking:

Moderator – Dr Mike Jones (Naarm/Melbourne, and lutruwita/Tasmania) is an archivist, historian, and researcher at the University of Tasmania, and inaugural Convenor of the Australian Society of Archivists' Research and Education Special Interest Group (REDSIG).

Dr Rose Barrowcliffe is the inaugural First Nations Archives Advisor to Queensland State Archives, and a Macquarie University Fellowship for Indigenous Researchers (MUFIR) post-doctoral research fellow in the Department of Critical Indigenous Studies at Macquarie University who researches the rights and representation of Indigenous peoples in archives.

Dr Eva Samaras (Naarm/Melbourne) is a records and information Senior Analyst at the University of Melbourne and an information studies Sessional Academic at Charles Sturt University.

Elliot Freeman (Naarm/Melbourne) is an archivist at La Trobe University, a doctoral candidate at Monash University, and a committee member of both the Australian Queer Archives (AQuA) and the Australian Society of Archivists' Victorian Branch.

Duncan Loxton is an archivist and the Senior Specialist in Data Curation at the UTS Library (University of Technology Sydney).

Annie Cameron is a non-indigenous linguist and archivist who works supporting Aboriginal language activities in the Pilbara region of Western Australia, and a PhD candidate in Information Systems at Charles Darwin University.

Dr James Lowry (Tandanya/Adelaide, settler on Matinecock land) is an Associate Professor at Queens College, City University of New York, where he is Chair of the Graduate School of Library and Information Studies.

---

*Correspondence: Mike Jones, Email: info@mikejonesonline.com

Moderator – Rachel Tropea (Naarm/Melbourne) is an archivist and the Senior Coordinator at RMIT University Archives, and a Co-organiser of Australasia Preserves and the Critical Archives Reading Group (Melb).

Conversation

Mike Jones: Thank you everyone for joining us today. We would like to start by asking about research and practice in your own work. Do you see a distinction between the two? What's the value of combining these elements, what are some of the challenges or barriers involved, and how have the different institutional contexts you have worked in shaped your response?

Rose Barrowcliffe: It's interesting, when I started working in archives my head was very much in a research space and I was surprised by how little awareness there was about what was happening in the research world around archives. I try to bring current work and current publications into the conversations with my work in archives, so obviously I think there's huge value in bringing those two elements together. The whole idea of scholarship is that it is the leading edge of knowledge. You're creating new knowledge, and if that's not being conveyed across into practice then there's not really much point.

MJ: Have you found any resistance from an institutional point of view?

RB: Not to the ideas, but there are funding timelines, and there are already things in the works, like the task list for the year. For example, we just went through a legislative review process here in Queensland. We have a new Public Records Act and through the stakeholder engagement workshops – which included Indigenous people, most of them working in government, and a lot of Queensland Government workers – we were trying to talk to them about, for example, Indigenous data, data sovereignty, and Indigenous cultural and intellectual property.

There's a lot of lip service around those issues in the government and in the archive. But when you try to talk about practical ways that they can be implemented, you hear a lot of 'Oh, well, we couldn't possibly do that', or 'That wouldn't work within the legislation'. I don't think that they would think they're resistant, but I think that the adoption of these sorts of principles (that can be quite esoteric in some ways) is quite minimal. People still hold on to the idea that 'In practice, we do it this way, because we've always done it this way'.

MJ: Eva, how about the environments that you've worked in?

Eva Samaras: I think I've been fortunate to end up in fairly research-based roles when I was in government. I found that they embraced and wanted more rigorous, evidence-based approaches, which was good because I didn't want to spend time working on something if it wasn't going to be effective. At the National Archives, they embrace research, and I was in a research-focussed department when I was working there. But at the same time, many government archives are grossly underfunded. I could roll out a program or do a piece of research, but they couldn't sufficiently fund the work. For example, often the projects I worked on would rely on my ability to access literature using my university logins. So, it's this situation where they really want it, but they are not always able to fund it properly.

That was something I found in the government space. Now, I'm in a university space, and I have more means to do the research. But I'm very much in a practitioner-focussed role right now, and my business as usual (BAU) takes up most of my time. In my current role, I am kept very busy advising people across the university. Digital processes and systems are the focus, making sure they are compliant with legislation and standards, so I don't really get to bring research into that space very often.

Presently in my work, I would say research is more like a side thing. Although, that being said, I've been recently working on a review project to examine a key information system at the University of Melbourne. I'm doing that with my manager who identified the opportunity to heavily draw upon my formal research experience in the review's undertaking. I designed the data collection and analysis approach, drafted the interview questionnaire and I wrote up the report that will go to the University Executive. So, because of my research background, they've been really happy to have me on board and help with that side of things. Overall, I'd say research is embraced but it's very much reliant on adequate resourcing and funding, which in my experience has not always been that great.

MJ: And in your BAU role, do you still see the research work that you've done as informing your day-to-day practice? Or is it something that only exists in roles that are explicitly identified as research-based?

ES: I think it's more the latter. It comes into play if I'm trying to communicate with stakeholders and explain, for example, 'what is an archive?' to try and help them understand the value of their records. They are thinking, 'why do we care about this?' and I have to try and explain. But it's like a simplified version of archival theory and principles. So, I don't really get into the research and theory much in my recent roles. I can't have those conversations now like I used to be able to have at Public Record Office Victoria (PROV) where you can have discussions to get right into the theory behind provenance or appraisal and share recently published academic papers around. I haven't been able to do things like that for a while.

MJ: Elliot, how would you respond to this wearing both your La Trobe University hat and your AQuA hat?

Elliot Freeman: I was working in archives even when I was doing my Master's, so I've been practising throughout my entire research career and all through my PhD. Research and practice have always sat side-by-side in my work.

It's really interesting actually, contrasting a community archive space versus an institutional archive space in terms of how research is applied or engaged with. Both are often very limited in what they can implement because of resource issues. It's been really interesting to see how little of the research being done in the community archives space actually comes into the day-to-day praxis, because it is a matter of just trying to do as much as you can as quickly as possible with so few resources – particularly with relatively few people volunteering who are trained archivists.

In the university space, we're an archive in a library. Much like Eva, I've done a lot of very bare bones education – 'Welcome to archives. We have boxes of stuff!' – as a way of trying to advocate for our work on the one hand, and then to push best practice on the other. When we redeveloped our collection development framework, I think we ended up putting in maybe three paragraphs about our participatory approach to our work, and we were asked why we'd included it. It seemed like such a valuable thing to include in the documentation: our perspective, our viewpoint, and the theoretical foundation for our work. And there was a little bit of, not resistance, but *uncertainty* as to the relevance of these sections and why we dedicated ink to it. That's been an ongoing discussion. I think it's important for us to explain that there is value in engaging with new thinking, and in reflecting on *why* we do the things we do, and not just *what* we do. And that's something I'm trying to implement more proactively in my own work in the community archives space – the why, as well as the what.

MJ: And in the community archives space do you see the relevance of theories of community archiving? Or is there a gap between practice and existing theoretical discussions around community archiving?

EF: In my experience, I think there's definitely a gap between that research and practice. A lot of the focus (as it should be) has been on broader issues of inclusion – for instance, around First Nations inclusion and disability inclusion – and that's been more the focus than archival theoretical perspectives. Looking to queer archival research specifically, as we continue working towards a digital collection management system at AQuA, I can see the relevance of some of that research coming in. For instance, that's when we tap into some of those broader international discussions, like the work that's been done at the Digital Transgender Archive,[1] the Homosaurus[2] and projects like that. But we're just quite not at that point yet.

MJ: Duncan, how does this play out in your work?

Duncan Loxton: I have been a practitioner my entire career. I've not been a researcher, but I am a bit of a gushing fan of research; and so I'd like to say that there isn't a distinction and that my work mirrors the leading edge of the best research that Rose was talking about, but that wouldn't be the whole truth. I find, perhaps because of the context that I'm working in, that I have a bit of trouble separating the two. But in listening to what Elliot was saying – the research is *why* we do things, and perhaps the professional practice is *how* we do things – then it's easier to make that distinction. In terms of the 'why', I point to research, I listen to researchers speaking, I read their papers when I get the time, and I use that as a source of inspiration, as well as the basis for change in our work. I'll try and make sure that it's always informing what we're doing and justifies the recommendations for change that I'm making when it goes up to be approved by a committee.

So I look to research for ideas that resonate with me. I'll often find that there's a question that I've been grappling with and someone's put it to words or explained it way better than I could so I'll cite that, and then that will change my frame of reference. I think Eva was saying that there's a bit of a challenge in translation sometimes, and there may not be the opportunity or the resourcing to do that translation work. I reflect that now I've been working at the same place for some time, and it's always been encouraged to engage with research. We support researchers, so we speak the language of research.

MJ: You say that you look to research to support the work that you want to do. When you go looking, do you ever find the research isn't there, or do you find the research you need is generally available?

DL: Generally, there's always something there. There's 20, maybe 30 years, perhaps even longer, of discussion about Indigenous sovereignty. If there's a question I need answering it's often there, and I actually find there's too much research. So I'll read a paper, then revisit it a year later and something else will jump out at me. Or I'll follow a reference in that paper and uncover something new. I've always been able to find something adjacent to the question that I'm asking. There will be something there reflecting that need that I have to articulate something that I've not been able to articulate before.

MJ: Annie, how about you?

Annie Cameron: There's definitely an overlap between research and practice. But I've come to archives as a language researcher, essentially, whose work was always slightly frustrated because of archival issues, so I often approach archive practice and research from that perspective. I work as a linguist at Wangka Maya Pilbara Aboriginal Language Centre, and I'm doing my PhD research on the archive there. My PhD was designed to fulfil the need for an archivist in the organisation so my research was always intended to meet very practical needs within the language centre. In terms of the value for the organisation, practice and research operates on a sliding scale. We can move it to a very practical position: the linguist just needs to be doing linguistics and getting that work done, which is our core business and will always be the priority. But having the 50:50 split between my daily job, and then my PhD research and being in the archive, we can also slide it all the other way and say: 'Okay, at the moment we're just doing 100% archival work, investigation, mobilising records for community use'.

The archive has accumulated so naturally and has evolved with what looks like a lot of disruption, but it's not disruption. It's just how the archive has come together through community creation and use over 35 years. Every time we use the archive we find out something new about it, so there's a very practical approach where we are doing language centre business, and we are finding out things about the archive as we do it, and I'm squirrelling those things away into the archive folders and thinking 'Oh, that's interesting!' It helps us understand what we can do to mobilise the language material in the archive to support activities in the community as needed.

The tension and challenge between the archive and the prioritisation of language work are always there, and we have to keep asking 'how can this support language learning?' That's the core business of the organisation. Language Centres have never received specific funding for their archives, and my PhD is the first archival research into a language centre archive in Australia. With my PhD coming to an end, we are developing strategies to make the archival work self-sustaining. The Language Centre operates under such robust Indigenous governance. One of the challenges for me as a non-Indigenous person with a researcher hat, and as an employee, is knowing where the parameters of what is in-house research that is just for the Language Centre, and what is able to be presented outside of the language centre context, or maybe just shared with other language centres that are also grappling with the same issues. My guidance comes from the rest of the team, who are Aboriginal, and the cultural authorities and board of directors. I discuss with them what I think are really important parts of the research output that could be shared more broadly with archival research communities beyond Language Centres, around Australia or around the world.

Part of the challenge also comes from linguistics, which historically has looked at language centre archives just as places where some language data are stored – a very practical computational or research repository infrastructure issue – whereas they're not. They're community based, Aboriginal-controlled archives that have very unique characteristics. In my research, I've become really aware of that, and wearing two hats, as a linguist and an archivist, can be a bit tricky in that situation.

MJ: Is there anything about archival theory and research that surprised you when you first started moving into that space from the linguistic space?

AC: I don't think there was much that surprised me. I mean, I finally got to understand the Australian Series system which has always been this mysterious thing out there that I didn't know, so that was really interesting for me. I also got to understand Australia's position globally as a place that's generated really useful archival theory and has made a significant contribution to the way that Indigenous materials are approached and treated in archival theory.

I trained in archives and records hoping it would help me understand how to manage Aboriginal community language archives better. During training, I saw that continuum theory was similar to the workflow of a language centre archive. The process of language documentation, language description, and then the activation of those records for language activities in a community, is also essentially a continuum that can't end. In my PhD, I've been able to understand that similarity at a far more practical and granular level. Not that the continuum is the answer to the perpetual problems of language centre archives, but I've been exploring whether the model provides a different way of looking at language centre archives and the work that produces them that we haven't used before.

What surprised me more is that in language centres – which are not a new thing in Australia, they've been around since the late 1980s – no language centre I've come across yet has had an archivist. They have these incredible, unique collections of community-created material. Wangka Maya represents 31 languages. The archive is so rich with linguistic, cultural, and historical material created by the community. The archive also contains material that has been returned from mainstream archives where it has been deposited by researchers. The two sources of community-produced material and material copied from other archives combine at Wangka Maya as the central archive for the Pilbara language, culture and history. When the material is viewed as a whole in the language centre context it tells a very different story that can be understood through archival concepts like parallel provenance.

As far as managing the archive, linguists and IT engineers have all built databases based on principles of research repositories designed for researchers. Community people have written lists and lists of metadata and have shaped how the material is managed in really important ways. But a trained archivist has never come in and looked at it – not in *any* language centre that I've come across yet.

So the challenge has really been identifying that gap, and then finding ways to bridge it. That doesn't mean that archivists are the people doing the work because the language centre I work at is so robustly governed by the community. The language centre has to be sustainable and self-determination is embedded in all of the activities. That means every step of the way for practice and research I am thinking, 'how can I withdraw, as a non-Indigenous person so that an Indigenous person, one of my colleagues, sits in this place and does this task instead?' Applying archival concepts has definitely helped me understand the language archive in a way that better supports community autonomy.

James Lowry: I was thinking about this question in relation to teaching, where there's a balance between engaging students with new research and preparing them to do a job – it's a vocational degree – so that tension between research and practice is always there. It's built into our program at City University of New York (CUNY); we have the Intro to Archives class, which is totally theoretical. It's the history of the field, the principles, and the theory building that has been the focus of a lot of research lately. And then the other compulsory class for our students is basically the practice class where they're learning how to do the appraisal, how to do arrangement and description. A division is built into the structure of the program, which can make it difficult to show students the relationship between the two, unless they're taking both classes at the same time.

I teach the more theoretical class, and I try to stress that these are ideas that you can choose to take with you into practice, or not. And as the next generation of archivists, the students will decide what archival theory and practice will look like in the future, because the norms of practice will be established by the theories they apply in the repository, and they can generate new theories out of their practice.

As we've been having this conversation I've also been thinking about a chapter in *Research in the Archival Multiverse* by Luciana Duranti and Giovanni Michetti called 'The Archival Method'.[3] They talk about how every aspect of archival work is a research undertaking. When we're doing appraisal we are doing research. We're trying to figure out the significance of records, creators, and functions. Then, when we're doing arrangement, we're trying to uncover modes of organisation, the functions and activities of the creating body and how these fit together. That's historical research. When we do description, we're doing documentary analysis, right? So research is woven into all aspects of the work. And as Eva was speaking, I was thinking about how that also applies to records management. If you're developing classification schemes or doing any kind of process analysis, these are all research activities as well. That tension is absolutely there, but in other ways, the distinction is also blurry.

MJ: James you have worked in a variety of contexts – the US, Europe, Africa, the Caribbean, Australia. Do you find that this plays out in different ways in different contexts around the world? Or are these fairly common, shared relationships between theory and practice and research and practice?

JL: I don't know. Practices, concepts and professional cultures all vary a lot but I don't know about attitudes to research: it didn't come up much. Maybe it's more of a generational thing? When I was a practitioner, I think a lot of my mentors and colleagues were sceptical of research and theory, and were critical of the academic arm of the profession. But I'm encouraged that my students are excited about the theoretical aspects because they understand that the work that they're doing as archivists – selecting the materials that will survive; the representation of history – can't be severed from the intellectual currents in our societies. They understand that these are important questions. When I speak to them about some of the opposition to 'theory', students often speak very articulately about the threats of anti-intellectualism, and how we want to avoid falling into this trap of viewing archives as purely a rote, mechanical job. Everything that we're doing needs to be critiqued, and research helps us do that.

MJ: Does anyone else see a generational shift here? Thinking about the different people you have worked with, and the different environments you've worked in, do you think that things are changing over time?

EF: When I was first entering the profession, I definitely noticed that when I mentioned I was finishing my Masters or doing my PhD a very common response would be, 'Oh, God! The continuum stuff!' And that was the first thought people had about research. You could see the exasperation on their faces. But when I was teaching archival/record-keeping students, they were always really interested and really engaged; and even if they weren't always sure what the application would be, they found talking about the ideas really enjoyable.

I particularly saw this at Monash where I was teaching a mix of students from the library and archives and recordkeeping specialisations, and then more technical disciplines like data science or cybersecurity. So many of my students, across all disciplinary backgrounds, liked having those big discussions about the ethics of archives, the work that we do, and the contingencies and subjectivities of it. I think they quite liked unpacking these ideas even if they didn't always see the practical implications for their future careers, whereas when I've been in workplaces with people who have been in the field for quite a long time, they almost had the inverse. They had spent so long trying to deal with doing the practical work with so few resources they couldn't see how these highfalutin ideas would actually help ameliorate those really practical challenges. There's quite a lot of 'No Man's Land' in the middle at the moment – a balance between trying to enrich practice with ideas and research, and the need to moderate that with the fact that a lot of people are really under the pump in terms of their BAU.

RB: It's funny for me, because I came to archives as a user, and that was through an archive that's about my traditional country where I just didn't see us being represented in this archive. It was actually archival theory that saved me in that process because I started reading Dr Kirsten Thorpe's work, for example. And I was like, 'Oh, thank God!' I had the people managing this archive saying things like, 'Oh, well, it doesn't really apply to you because there's not really any cultural content to the records', things like that. Then to read people's work that brought in Indigenous perspectives through research – and not just Indigenous perspectives, but looking at queer theory and feminist theory, and looking at activist archives, particularly in the US – and being able to see another way of doing things. That's what really got me interested in archives. I think if I had just stopped after looking at the archive as it currently existed, I would never be doing what I'm doing today. So I totally changed my perception of archives by reading theory, and that was before I was an academic. And then through that, I ended up enrolling in my post-grad degree.

MJ: Extending from that, Rose and Duncan, you are part of the Indigenous Archives Collective (IAC).[4] How do you see the role of a group like that in both influencing practice and bringing more theoretical understandings to these spaces?

RB: For me, it's been hugely influential personally, but I also see the impact of the work of that collective across the profession. Duncan runs or coordinates all these things, so props to Duncan. But those get-togethers are really nourishing spaces as well. I think for the people who are part of the collective, if you're working in a space where you're seeing a big disconnect between what you would like to see happening in practice and what is actually happening in practice, it's a great space to go in and let off steam, share experiences, and be inspired by other people's work. And there are a lot of people in the collective who are across practice and academia in some capacity or other – not necessarily studying, but who might be working in university archives, or like Duncan who is a practitioner at the university. I think it's really important, the work that the IAC does.

DL: I became involved with the Collective because of my role working with the Aboriginal and Torres Strait Islander Data Archive (ATSIDA) and some of the people in the collective. I got to know them and became interested in their work, and thought that I should be supporting them in ways beyond just the reach of the data archive that I work in. The Collective is a place in which I can offer additional support and advice.

I think I'm fortunate to have worked at the University for 10 years. That's given me time to come to grips with some of the ideas that the collective is often discussing, and it's meant that we've had time to see the outcomes of implementing some of those ideas. That's a luxury in many ways. If you can stick it out, you'll see the change that you want to see. I do value the Collective, and the conversations that happen, and I'm constantly astonished at the amount of work that's happening in this space – that integration of theory and practice, that leading edge that Rose was mentioning. I'm just full of admiration for the people in that Collective.

MJ: There are other structures in our profession that try and work to bring these areas together. There are the Australian Society of Archivists (ASA) conferences, where you get practitioners, theorists, and researchers in the same space. There are international archival conferences, there are journals like *Archives & Manuscripts*. There are branch meetings, branch events, and more. How do you think we're going as a sector and a profession, in terms of building a culture where research and practice are working together in useful ways?

ES: I have had quite a bit of exposure to the ASA conference and more recently Records and Information Management Practitioners Alliance (RIMPA) forum events. The ASA feels quite strong. I think the conference really does bring together a good mix of voices and issues – sometimes hard ones to deal with. I'm thinking of the last conference in particular, which was heavy at times (in a good way). I've only been attending on and off for the last few years, but I think the people involved in organising the ASA conferences are doing a good job, and it's getting better in that it's bringing important issues to the fore and featuring a good range of voices. RIMPA is more on the practical side of things from what I've seen. It's focussed on tools and emerging technologies and things like that which is still important, but it is not so heavy on the research. I don't feel like that's something that's explored in that space, from my experience.

One thing I do like about our sector is that a lot of our journals are open access by default, and there are many great blogs as well. I have also found organisations like the Digital Preservation Coalition (DPC)[5] helpful. The DPC shares the scholarship and research that they do proactively, both often and for free, and if you can pay as an institution you'll get access to even more. From my experience working in the sector, it's been quite good in that I have access to a lot of information and a lot of research when I need it, and I don't necessarily have to do that through my university access. I can also do it as a practitioner.

JL: I've been reading a lot of old back issues of some of the journals because I'm increasingly interested in the history of our field, and you can really see the way that the articles have moved from being descriptive, or reports about events and activities, into more formally structured research articles. The quality and the level of analysis have become much richer over time, and that is partly because of things like the growth of archival studies PhD programs, journals, and the Archival Education Research Institute (AERI),[6] which started in the US but from its earliest days included a strong contingent of Australian participants. The field building and the scholarly infrastructure that has been put in place by the senior academics, all of that has increased the rigour of the work and set higher expectations.

Thinking about Australia and the work that was being done in the 1960s at the National Archives or the Commonwealth Archives at that time, we could probably say that Australia has long been open to questioning. I think that's a key characteristic of Australian archival thinking: an openness to new ways of doing things generally. And that comes through in the journals and the conferences. Over the last few years, I have been a little sceptical about some of the newest continuum work, but at the same time, there are several other really exciting things happening in the Australian scene. There's the Indigenous data sovereignty work that others have spoken about. There's the trauma-informed work coming out of Melbourne. Rachel, your Critical Archives Reading Group[7] has stimulated a lot of new thinking as well. So it's always been there. But you can also chart a rise, an improvement.

MJ: Annie, as a relative newcomer to the profession, how do you find those professional structures?

AC: I am a newcomer to archives and I'm still becoming familiar with the current situation in Australia. I've jumped in at the deep end a bit through involvement in ASA committees which are very supportive of new members in my experience. I've come from linguistics which is a far smaller discipline, especially for so called Australianists, who specialise in Australian Aboriginal languages. So coming into archives, it seems very professionalised, and the sector is far more developed. It has longevity and also numbers – there's just more people – partly because records and archives are supported through legislation in all States and Territories. We don't have the regulatory aspect in Australian linguistics and I've noticed the research components of both disciplines speak to that.

It seems to me that, like James said, we have a long history of innovation in archives in Australia, and it's been really interesting to see. My feeling is that in linguistics it's kind of the opposite – it's a much more closed discipline in that sense. Over the last 6 months, I've been very interested in watching other linguists who don't have a background in archives, navigate archives. That's been an interesting experience because it's made me realise how familiar I've become with archives and archival theory, and how far we might have to go in archives to cross over into related disciplines. I'm not sure we're doing a lot of that kind of work at the moment. Maybe that's something we need to look at a bit more.

EF: I did take note of James's point about the latest continuum work. I did both my master's and my PhD at Monash, so my archival worldview has been really shaped by continuum thinking. And I've been having a lot of discussions as I come to the end of my PhD about articulating my relationship with continuum thinking from a methodological standpoint. Because it was day one of my archival education, it's been really foundational. It's the lens through which I see and think about archives, but it's so inherent that I'm not always conscious of it.

When I speak with other researchers working in spaces like queer archives and Indigenous archives, there's a lot of work being done to critically re-evaluate what we sometimes take for granted – those foundational elements of the discipline, the theory, or of our research. There are people trying to reconfigure those foundational elements in a new way, or in a different way based on our context now. It's a perspective that is often much more critical, especially from an inclusion and social justice perspective, which I think is for the better. It's going to be really interesting to see the next 5 or 10 years of research come out as hopefully those discussions become even more critical and reflexive and interrogative.

Rachel Tropea: Following on from what Elliot was saying about people's reactions to their PhD and the records continuum, archival theory often gets critiqued for being too complex or opaque. What are your thoughts on that?

DL: I often think reflexively, that it's my own lack of creativity and imagination that means that I can't comprehend what the research is, or what the researcher is trying to say to me, and so I'm sympathetic. But earlier I mentioned reading an article once, and then reading it a second time, and giving myself that space to come to grips with that research side. And so I suppose I can only be encouraging, which is part of my own self-talk. It's good to be patient, and not to give up right away.

RB: I definitely struggle with some of the denser theoretical stuff, but I'm not a linear learner. I need to go over things again and again and take a little bit more time. The continuum model is a key example of that. I avoided it as much as I could because I just found it too complex, and I couldn't understand it. And then I got to the last year of my PhD and I was looking for a framework to lay my analysis over. And all of a sudden it clicked, and I was like, 'Oh, I see now'. But I needed something to apply it to, I couldn't just read it as a theory in isolation from what I was trying to do. Like Duncan said, it takes time and patience sometimes; but I always appreciate that people have put a lot of thought into this, into anything they put down on paper, so I try to stick with it as much as possible.

JL: I think that theory and research can act on practice in a couple of ways. With a lot of the critical work coming out of the US for example, the authors will take an idea from, let's say, feminist theory, and then they'll work it through in terms of archival procedures. 'What if we take this idea and apply it to appraisal?' Those articles often end on a practical note: 'Here is what this might look like in practice'. So there you have a very direct relationship, and a lot of the translation work has been done by the authors.

But in other contexts – and I think the continuum is one – the influence of theory can work differently. If you're in a meeting, you're not going to start speaking to your boss about continuum theory because their eyes would glaze over. It's too complex and it's not directly translatable. On the other hand, it has precipitated some major shifts in the way that we think about the work we do. One example is the fact that the international records management standard treats appraisal not as a moment in a life cycle, but as a continuous activity that begins before the creation of a record. I think we can attribute that change in our understanding of appraisal to the thinking around the continuum model. There are different ways that research can translate into practice, at a very broad level, and then in a more direct way.

ES: I did my PhD with a cohort of people who weren't in my field. I found that quite interesting. My supervisor was not an archivist and was always asking questions, which was great, but it was often this process of trying to translate my whole profession to someone who had no knowledge about the area. Then as we continued that journey over three and a half years, by the end of it he started picking up on the terms, and he would say 'That's appraisal' and I'd say 'Yes!' and he'd say, 'I'm an archivist!' and I'm like, 'Maybe not!'

But I liked to see my colleagues starting to get it through me sharing my thesis chapters or journal papers with them and discussing papers in our reading club. We were a small cohort and would all share each other's work as we went along. I found that helpful in that it was a good opportunity to explain the theory, but in a different way, to a different audience. Being a researcher in a multi-disciplinary cohort forced me to find new ways of exploring and sharing archival theory, such as selecting papers to share in reading club that weren't necessarily directly about archiving, but were something on the peripheral that would engage them.

RT: Annie, you talked about crossing disciplines as well. Archival scholars have written about this and we often complain about how historians for example don't engage with archival theory when they write about archives. But perhaps it goes both ways?

AC: Like Eva was saying, I also don't have an archivist on my supervision panel so as a student, I've done some of that teaching archives and archival theory to a supervisor. And I do have an underlying anxiety that I'm possibly getting it all wrong! The continuum theory is complex but it's important for us to understand the circumstances that it came out of, and James has touched on that. I'm particularly interested in it because Peter J. Scott, who was at the Commonwealth Archives Office, was also a linguist before becoming an archivist. The underlying principles of what became the Commonwealth Records Series are really familiar to us as linguists, but I've asked around and no linguists I've spoken with have heard of Scott!

Working across linguistics and archives, I navigate language and translation between disciplines. When I talk to an IT team, I get so confused, but we're talking about the same thing essentially, we're just using different words. And when I talk to linguists now, they're getting confused because I'm talking like an archivist, but we're talking about the same thing again. Finding that common language and being clear on definitions is part of approaching the complexity of theory.

I've been thinking a lot recently about the conversations that we're having about data and the conversations that we have about records, and how these two things are often conflated; maybe without even realising sometimes. But they are different things, and they need to be treated differently. We have to maintain those definitions when we're having conversations across disciplines as well. There are a lot of linguists doing archiving but not many of them are trained in archives, and even fewer know continuum theory. Yes, the theory is complex, but I think the starting point for speaking with non-archivists might be, 'Do you know there is a theory?' We need to remind people that it's not just archivists filing stuff in cardboard boxes in the back rooms of organisations. There are really strong, underlying principles through which we approach our work.

EF: I'm going to call myself out here: I think I am often guilty of conflating research and theory when I speak about the relationship between research and practice. As James said, there is a lot of research that in varying degrees is prescriptive, but is certainly more grounded in direct, practical applications. And I've been reflecting on this as both a researcher and a practitioner as I'm finalising my PhD, thinking about what I am producing that is actually of practical benefit to the profession. Doing a queer PhD, I'm very mindful of that because – how do I say this? – a lot of queer research can tend towards the slightly *esoteric*. And so for a lot of archival practitioners, it can be a little bit dense and hard to implement and hard to see the value.

I was writing the other day and I described what I'm trying to produce as something like a menu that archivists can use to order what they can afford and what they have the stomach for. It doesn't have to be 'absolute truth from God'. It's about trying to create practical tools that people can actually engage with, think about, and apply.

I've had a lot of discussions recently about the conflation of research and theory, and maybe that turns some people off. They think that anything to do with research is a continuum-level dense, philosophical exegesis that is a little bit impenetrable. Yet sometimes research is exceedingly practical and really straightforward, and can just be something you refer to if you have a question you need answered.

RT: Archives are not neutral spaces, and are not just for the preservation of records. They are there for access and use. Sometimes they can also stand in the way of access, and that can have significant implications for communities. So what does all this talk of theory, research, and practice mean for users of archives? Is it a distinction that has any relevance to users and communities? Rose, you said you started your journey as a user of archives.

RB: Yes, and that's exactly where my answer starts. I saw the usefulness for myself as a user. I work across or with a few large collecting institutions and one of the frustrations for users is that they have to learn a new language or a new system every time they go to a different institution. But to them they just want to find their stuff – they shouldn't have to relearn everything. It's similar to theory, in that our role as people who sit across these spaces is to translate it to the user so they don't have to become experts in all of the theories themselves. We should be able to explain it in a way that they could understand so they can find their stuff. I mean, that's the goal right? Find and use their stuff. And for me, an example of that is Indigenous standpoint theory. It really helped me to be able to look at archives and archival practice in a way that meant I could see how this would impact the user and recognise why things need to change in certain ways for Aboriginal and Torres Strait Islanders who use archives so that users are able to find their stuff.

ES: This is a gap in my experience because I'm not a user of archives. But I think about users, especially when I do descriptive work. For example, when I worked at PROV I took a different approach to writing series descriptions, applying accessible language and more summarised information because I found some existing descriptions to be too dense. I thought 'most people just want to know what the records are, we don't have to give them a full history about everything'.

Like Rose was saying, in terms of users having to relearn – especially when a user comes up with a barrier and questions 'Why aren't I allowed to access these records? What are my rights as a user? What is the kind of framework that's operating?' – then they might start getting a bit into the theory. Potentially also looking at legislation, because the legislation is different in every jurisdiction (which is so annoying), and the way that access is provided also differs. I am still perplexed by how the National Archives manages access. It's not scalable. It's not practical, especially in the digital world. As a non-user, I presume theory might come into play more when a user's hand is forced, and they must acquire deeper knowledge to be able to work the system.

JL: All of the research and theory and everything else that we've been speaking about today absolutely shapes what the user will encounter in the archive in terms of what's present or absent, how it's represented in the finding aids – all of that kind of stuff. But I feel like there's something to be said about how the knowledge the user is bringing to the archive is quite important, not just for their meaning-making in the archive, but how we think about our core concepts. For example, Sony Prosper's work on how community attitudes might help us conceptualise what a record is.[8] Users are part of the research/practice mix in under-recognised ways.

DL: I've never been a user of archives, but when I'm reading theory or when I'm reading research it offers me a window into archival practice somewhere else. And so I'll see the winds of change, you know? I'll see what best practice looks like in another area of Australia, and I'll get people who will start to prepare me at least intellectually, and start driving me to improve our offering locally because I think people's experiences change the more they interact with archives. Engaging with that research is good for the user as a sort of proxy for my own archive. But I don't remember anyone pointing to a piece of research and approaching us as an archive.

EF: In my research I've interviewed a number of people – queer historians primarily – who go into institutional archives, national, state, and university collections, trying to find things and they absolutely have to become experts in archives in order to find those materials. The skill sets that they have to acquire are incredible, just to be able to navigate collections and find what they need.

What I found interesting was that while they had this immense practical knowledge of how collections are structured and how to navigate them, there was sometimes not a full understanding of the biases and contingencies of those systems. I think there was still a surprising amount of faith in how those records were described, arranged, and managed, and maybe less awareness of the imperfections of archival systems and the human beings doing the work. So that was a really interesting contrast.

AC: I've been thinking so much recently about access and use of the language centre archive because the people who mostly access it are the same people and families that created the material in it, and that have run the organisation that the archive sits within, and that have managed non-Aboriginal people coming in – mostly linguists and researchers. So access looks totally different from what we're used to as archivists in mainstream settings. I've had to really rejig the way I think about access and use.

A huge component of my PhD thesis is about the language material that was created before Wangka Maya that is held in mainstream archives. I didn't plan for that to become a focus, but it had to be. I examined every major archival language collection from the first expedition into the Pilbara up to 1987. I was able to identify each language and person in all that material. That shouldn't have been work that Wangka Maya had to dedicate resources to, the material is held by institutions that receive funding for archiving. I know it's not enough funding, but they receive a huge amount of funding compared to what any community language centre is ever going to receive for their archive. However, my work was done through Wangka Maya, so the material belongs there now, in the community it came from. I can see what could happen is that the archives that hold the material will want access to that information to improve their collection metadata and inform access protocols. It will be up to Wangka Maya to really decide what to do with the information and how to negotiate that process.

Generally, access is simple and well established within the community, because material created since 1987 was created with a clear purpose at Wangka Maya. Material created before Wangka Maya is understood in the community as being created for the same purpose and treated with the same access protocols. The Pilbara is such a unique region historically and that is reflected in the continuity of language and culture, throughout the community and in the archive.

RT: One final question, what are some practical steps or an action we could take as a profession to improve the way theory and practice work together in archives?

ES: When I finished my PhD I felt like I was a bit disconnected from scholarship. I was going back to work full-time. So, I participated in the Critical Archives Reading Group. I found it helpful to activate my brain in an academic way and engage with other archivists about ideas and practice. I encourage people to join. It's a great group.

DL: I was reflecting on my comments about reading all this research, and thinking that I work in a university that has *access* to a whole lot of research. We have subscriptions to all these channels and databases, and that makes it readily available to me. So I'd encourage anyone who doesn't have that kind of access to seek out the authors of the research if they can. Find their email and get in touch with them, because they'll often be able to provide you with a copy of their research, and they would be thrilled that you're interested in their research. And of course, there are other places to find research online. For example, institutional repositories will often publish versions of research before they go to print so you'll be able to access pretty much the same thing for free.

EF: What I try and do is think about how engaging with research can help educate me and help me to take on the burden of self-education, particularly in my position as an able-bodied person, as a white person, as a person living in a colonised state. I think about how research can help to expand my knowledge, improve my practice, and not rely on colleagues within those positionalities to take on that burden themselves. I think we're really lucky to be in a context in Australia where incredibly diverse research is coming out that can help you do that work. Even if you just read one paper a month on a lunch break, and just start really thinking critically about the work you do and how you can help support necessary changes in how we think about and do archival work.

JL: For me, there are three things that come to mind. First, I think the open access stuff that Duncan mentioned is really important. I'm really proud that *Archives & Manuscripts* has moved in that direction. That's valuable, and I think we have to normalise it as an expectation more and more wherever possible. I would love to see *Archival Science* fully open access. I'm co-editing a book series and those books are expensive, so I understand that it's a little ironic that I'm saying this, but I do think that open access is an important part of this.

If we want more reciprocity or more interaction between research and practice, then we need to consider research design and research methods, as core competencies for archival work and build that into whatever kind of education programs we're designing. I know that's a problem in Australia at the moment, with the education situation looking a bit bleak, but however training or education is happening, research skills should be part of it.

And then the reverse of that is a problem I'm seeing in North America that I don't think exists in Australia, which is this pipeline from the Master's degree straight into the PhD and then straight into academic jobs. You've got people who are writing and teaching about archival studies without ever having been a practitioner. I think that that shows up in their understanding of the work and raises a question about how informed their teaching is. So I think it works both ways. We want practising archivists to be researchers, but we also need the archival educators to engage with practice really solidly.

RB: One of the things that the ASA Queensland Branch and Queensland State Archives (QSA) do really well, is that they host talks regularly from researchers at the archives where practitioners can come and hear about the latest research. I think that's a really good way to do it. But yeah, open access all the way!

AC: I agree about publications being open access absolutely; but also presentations and talks. I'm often looking up archives and records talks on YouTube and I'm very appreciative that over the history of archives in Australia, YouTube has been a platform that's been used a lot.

Archives still have that regulatory function in government, and something we've discussed at the WA State Branch has been the diminishing number of people participating in the ASA. Even people who are at the Specified Calling Level in the public service as archives or records managers are not necessarily participating or holding membership in the professional bodies. Whether that's a government sector trend or a trend that ASA and RIMPA are looking at, I think that might be something that we need to approach; and as a profession, especially as a profession that does have a regulatory function, we need to make sure that professional development is active. Also, we need to support research practice in the workplace. Like James said, so much of the archival process involves on-the-job research, so we really need to maintain an understanding of that which I'm not seeing so much in younger professionals. The older generation of professionals is reaching retirement and commitment to the profession and on-the-job research is not necessarily carrying through.

RT: Thank you so much for your time, it's been absolutely fascinating.

Notes on contributors

Dr Mike Jones is an archivist, historian, and collections consultant with more than 15 years of experience working with the GLAM sector (galleries, libraries, archives, and museums) on digital, archival, and public history projects. Mike's interdisciplinary research explores the history of archives and museums, and the ways in which collections-based knowledge is documented, managed, exhibited, and preserved, with a particular interest in the potential of contemporary technologies to support this work. He is currently a Postdoctoral Fellow – Indigenous and Colonial Histories (University of Tasmania), and inaugural Convenor of the Australian Society of Archivists' Research and Education Special Interest Group (REDSIG). Mike is the author of *Artefacts, Archives, and Documentation in the Relational Museum* (Routledge, 2022).

Dr Rose Barrowcliffe is a Butchulla postdoctoral research fellow at the Department of Indigenous Studies and the Centre for Global Indigenous Futures. Rose's research examines the representation of Indigenous peoples in archives at both an organisational level and a record level. Rose is the inaugural First Nations Archives Advisor to the QSA and is an active member of the IAC.

Dr Evanthia (Eva) Samaras is a practitioner-researcher specialising in information management, archiving, digital preservation and media production. She presently works in the Information Governance Services group at the University of Melbourne and previously held positions at the National Archives of Australia, PROV and the Australian Broadcasting Corporation. Eva completed her PhD in 2021 at the University of Technology Sydney. Her research examines records and archiving practices in the global film and television visual effects industry.

Elliot Freeman is an archival researcher and practitioner in Naarm/Melbourne. In the final stages of her doctorate at Monash University, Elliot's research explores queer/ing reparative description in institutional archives. She presently works as an archivist at La Trobe University and has a particular interest in making archival collections, skillsets, and experiences accessible for students. Elliot is a committee member of both the AQuA and the Australian Society of Archivists' Victorian Branch.

Duncan Loxton is an archivist involved in scholarly communication and managing research data. Duncan works for the Aboriginal and Torres Strait Islander Data Archive (ATSIDA) at the University of Technology Sydney Library where he strives to support the individual and collective rights of researchers, community groups and institutions to control the circumstances in which their knowledge is shared and applied. Duncan has previously worked at the Australian Museum, and State Archives and Records NSW.

Annie Cameron has worked with Aboriginal communities in the Pilbara region of Western Australia since 2014. She has extensive experience in language documentation, description and language revitalisation and maintenance. Annie completed her graduate diploma in archives and records management at Curtin in 2020 followed by a brief stint in public recordkeeping. Annie works closely with Pilbara Aboriginal community members to support the development of local linguistic and archival practices. She is currently the Senior Linguist at Wangka Maya Pilbara Aboriginal Language Centre. Annie's PhD at Charles Darwin University is investigating how an Aboriginal language centre archive supports community language activities.

Dr James Lowry is an Associate Professor and current Chair of the Graduate School of Library and Information Studies, Queens College, CUNY. James is the Ellen Libretto and Adam Conrad Endowed Chair in Information Studies and the founder and director of the Archival Technologies Lab. He is an Honorary Research Fellow at University College London and the University of Liverpool, where he was co-director of the Centre for Archive Studies, following a career in record-keeping in Australia, Europe, Africa and the Caribbean. His recent publications include *Disputed Archival Heritage*, an edited collection published by Routledge in 2022 and, with Riley Linebaugh, the award-winning article 'The Archival Colour Line: Race, Records and Post-Colonial Custody'. His writing has been translated into French, Spanish and Portuguese. James is the convenor of *Archival Discourses*, an international research network that fosters critical enquiry into the intellectual history of archives, and he is co-editor of the *Routledge Studies in Archives* book series.

Rachel Tropea is the Archivist and Senior Coordinator at RMIT University Archives. Prior to this, she was a research archivist at the University of Melbourne. Most of Rachel's experience has been in the 'action research' space, working on nationwide projects involving the community, practitioners, and researchers. This includes the *Who Am I?* and *Find & Connect* projects with people who grew up in out-of-home care in their quest to find out about their childhood, and, on another project, with Aboriginal and Torres Strait Islander people to repatriate ancestral remains from museums, collecting institutions (including universities) and private collections, back to their community of origin.

Notes

1. Digital Transgender Archive, available at https://www.digitaltransgenderarchive.net/, accessed 4 June 2024.
2. Homosaurus—An international LGBTQ+ linked data vocabulary, available at https://homosaurus.org/, accessed 4 June 2024.
3. Luciana Duranti and Giovanni Michetti, 'The Archival Method,' in Anne J. Gilliland, Sue McKemmish, and Andrew J. Lau (eds.), Research in the Archival Multiverse, Monash University Publishing, Clayton, Victoria, 2017, pp. 75–95.
4. Indigenous Archives Collective, available at https://indigenousarchives.net/, accessed 4 June 2024.
5. Digital Preservation Coalition, available at https://www.dpconline.org/, accessed 4 June 2024.
6. Archival Education Research Institute, available at https://aeri.website/, accessed 4 June 2024.
7. Critical Archives Reading Group, available at https://www.criticalarchivesreading.com/, accessed 4 June 2024.
8. 'Theodore Calvin Pease Award: Sony Prosper,' Society of American Archivists, 2023, available at https://www2.archivists.org/recipients/theodore-calvin-pease-award-sony-prosper, accessed 4 June 2024.

ARTICLE

Designing Indigenous-Led Archival Futures: The Application of Indigenous Research Methodologies Within Archival Research and Practice

Kirsten Thorpe*

Jumbunna Institute for Indigenous Research and Education, University of Technology Sydney, Sydney, Australia

Abstract

This paper discusses the role and importance of Indigenous research methodologies in building spaces for Indigenous-led archival futures in Australia. It considers the development of professional statements of support for advancing First Nations engagement and Indigenous self-determination in the archives as an example of where Indigenous research methodologies and methods can increase Indigenous agency and decision-making in the archives. The research design, methodologies and methods, including Yarning, Indigenous Standpoint and Indigenous Storywork, utilised in the research project *Unclasping the White Hand: Reclaiming and Refiguring the Archives to Support Indigenous Wellbeing and Sovereignty* are discussed to highlight the importance of bridging gaps between research and practice. In doing this, it describes pathways for building respectful and ethical research in partnership with First Nations people in Australia. It contributes to dialogue on how these approaches can support the decolonisation of archival research, which in turn has the power to build transformations of practice to support First Nations archival priorities.

Keywords: *Indigenous research methodologies*; *Indigenous archives*; *Indigenous research paradigm*; *Yarning methods*; *Indigenous Storywork*

It is hard to want self-determination in a system that is very Westernised. I think that is a problem. Archives and libraries are naturally, Western. They were not designed with First Nations sovereignty and First Nations self-determination in mind. They are things that we are trying to incorporate now. That is why it can be difficult for it to happen now, and hopefully it will happen in the future. But it will be a slow process … there are ways we can do it in small doses that are effective and good, but at the same time I think it also requires mass disruption, that organisations might not be ready for (Nathan Sentance, Wiradjuri).[1]

---

*Correspondence: Kirsten Thorpe, Email: kirsten.thorpe@uts.edu.au

This paper considers how pathways to support First Nations' sovereignty and self-determination in the archives require institutions and professional associations to move beyond symbolic statements and instead commit to disrupting the status quo in archival practice. The application of Indigenous research methodologies is discussed as a tool to reimagine more culturally appropriate practices in the archives. The development of institutional and professional statements of support that are formulated through Indigenous ways of knowing, being and doing would establish reciprocal relationships between institutions, the professions and First Nations communities. An Indigenous-led and community-driven approach has the potential to bring mutual benefits for all involved. In exploring these ideas, the paper highlights the critical role of Indigenous research methodologies in building spaces for Indigenous-led archival futures to support the decolonisation of archival practice.

The first section reflects on the broad context of global movements to support Indigenous agency and decision-making in the archives. It highlights examples of Australian leadership in this global movement, including the development of the Australian Society of Archivists (ASA) (1996) *Policy Statement on Archival Services and Aboriginal and Torres Strait Islander Peoples*.[2] It then outlines the calls to action articulated in the International Council on Archives (ICA) *Tandanya-Adelaide Declaration* (2019). As reference points for discussing First Nations priorities, decision-making and sovereignty, the statements are utilised to identify gaps and opportunities to strengthen and activate the statements through Indigenous-led research agendas. This is followed by discussion of the principles set by the international Indigenous Data Sovereignty (IDS) movement, highlighting the need for more significant connections to be forged between these principles and archival scholarship and practice.

Next, I turn to my own research to reflect on how stepping away from professional practice and engaging in a sharp turn to research has been a significant form of empowerment to raise awareness of Indigenous priorities in the archives. I describe the approaches and methods utilised in my doctoral research project *Unclasping the White Hand: Reclaiming and Refiguring the Archives to Support Indigenous Wellbeing and Sovereignty*,[3] including Yarning, Indigenous Standpoint and Indigenous Storywork. In describing the research, I consider the effectiveness of Indigenous research methodologies in supporting disruption and change to reshape archival futures for First Nations people. I explore how these methods can enable Indigenous-led approaches to memory keeping, archiving and information exchange.

Through this, the paper responds to critical questions: How can Indigenous research methodologies support Indigenous self-determination in archives? What is the relationship between research and practice to achieve these goals? How can research design and methods model more effective approaches to archives and contribute to innovation in Indigenous research methodologies? Finally, I suggest pathways for archivists to build ethical approaches to respond to these situations within practice appropriately. I then return to the importance of the archives engaging further with the IDS movement to effect change at a community level.

National and international calls for Indigenous self-determination in the archives

Archival self-determination enables First Nations people to have control over decision-making about the stewardship, management and use of materials relating to their histories and cultures. The calls for Indigenous archival self-determination have grown nationally and internationally over the past three decades.[4] The grass-roots movement for Indigenous rights has been hard-fought, community-led and waged for generations. The 2007 *United Nations Declaration on the Rights of Indigenous Peoples* (UNDRIP) consolidated international recognition of the aspiration of Indigenous people to control their cultural heritage materials, including within archives. Also, in this period, First Nations stories about encounters with the archives became more prominent.

In Australia, the voices of Indigenous researchers, historians, creative practitioners and information and archive workers have described the negative experiences of engaging with racist, offensive and biased colonial collections.[5] The stories recount the tensions of people connecting with materials written from the perspective of government, church authorities or official actions rather than those of Indigenous people. First Nations people have described the emotional pain and distress of accessing collections that are discomforting, unsafe and make people feel ill-at-ease.[6] The negative impacts of Indigenous people engaging with colonial archives documenting massacres, the removal of children and other similar traumatic events have become more apparent. The colonial systems of archiving are under the spotlight as instruments of pain and trauma. First Nations people have described how colonial archiving systems breach cultural protocols, and Indigenous people feel distressed when they have accessed materials containing Indigenous knowledges meant for only certain people in the community[7] – for example, secret and sacred materials or other materials collected without informed consent or the adequate protection of Indigenous Cultural and Intellectual Property (ICIP) rights.[8] The growing literature, including my own research outlined later in this paper, explores how accessing records can cause harm to Indigenous people, ranging from Indigenous archives and information workers to those who access and use materials in physical or digital archive spaces. This increased awareness has highlighted the fact that the lack of First Nations control of the archives negatively impacts Indigenous people's wellbeing. At the same time, the stories demonstrate the critical importance of Aboriginal and Torres Strait Islander people accessing information about family and land ties for piecing histories of dispossession and removal back together, and speak of the value of people witnessing records of resistance and advocacy by First Nations people in the face of discriminatory government policies.[9]

Demand has been placed on archival institutions to respond and build engagement with First Nations people to address these tensions. Archival institutions and the broader information professions nationally and internationally have responded with various statements, protocols and frameworks for action to improve archival practice.[10] In Australia, the ground-breaking *Protocols for Libraries, Archives and Information Services* developed in 1995 by the Aboriginal and Torres Strait Islander Library, Information and Resource Network (ATSILIRN) spearheaded a movement for libraries, archives and information services to engage with First Nations people and priorities meaningfully.[11] The ASA then endorsed the ATSILIRN Protocols and guidelines for use with the profession in 1996 in their *Policy Statement on Archival Services and Aboriginal and Torres Strait Islander Peoples*. The ASA Policy Statement brought national attention to the role of records in the reconciliation process in Australia. The statement encouraged a new wave of action and support for First Nations people in the archives, recognising the importance of Aboriginal and Torres Strait Islander people being connected with the profession and being actively involved in archival planning and decision-making about the operation of the archives. Notably, the statement recognised the offensive and insensitive nature of the content of the records. It encouraged a new focus on the design of systems and services that would provide a less discomforting and more welcoming (or in the words of the statement, 'relatively stress-free') engagement for First Nations people entering the archives nationally.[12]

Internationally, the writings of Indigenous archival scholars Allison Boucher Krebs,[13] Jennifer O'Neal[14] and Raymond Frogner[15] describe the history and depth of work undertaken to forge Indigenous archive agendas within Indigenous contexts. Similarly, within the allied library and information science fields, Indigenous scholars have examined the intersection of library and information science and practice with Indigenous knowledges, considering questions of research ethics, relational research and the implementation of Indigenous protocols.[16] Collective groups including the International Indigenous Librarian's Forum (IIFL) led conversations on the importance of Indigenous self-determination across library, archive and information services. Significant leadership for the development of IIFL was provided by Te Rōpū Whakahau, the leading national body representing Māori people engaged with Libraries, Culture, Knowledge, Information, Communication and Systems Technology in Aotearoa/New Zealand, the organisation of the first gathering of IILF took place in 1999.[17] Elsewhere, professional associations developed protocols and statements to support better access to collections for Indigenous people and greater control of materials according to Indigenous protocols. For example, in the United States, the First Archivists Circle developed the *Protocols for Native American Archival Materials* (2008), bringing significant debate on Indigenous priorities within the Society of American Archivists.[18] In Canada, the Association of Canadian Archivists responded to archival agendas identified in the 2015 Report of the Truth and Reconciliation Commission of Canada (TRC). The TRC reporting recommended that the archives examine the extent to which institutions had complied with the UNDRIP and produce a report with recommendations on its full implementation.[19] Also, in that year, the *Reconciliation Framework: The Response to the Report of the Truth and Reconciliation Commission Taskforce* developed an in-depth pathway for archives to support systemic change in the archives for Indigenous people. Their report notes that 'archives and archivists need a tangible way to move beyond the confines of a harmful, racist system of professional practice'.[20]

The development of the ICA's Tandanya-Adelaide Declaration (2019) brings the calls for Indigenous self-determination in archives into sharp focus. As a guiding document, the declaration represents a culmination of the work of the broader movement of recognising Indigenous worldviews and rights in libraries and archives. Importantly, the declaration advocates for a paradigm shift in traditional archival practice to develop a 'new model of public archives as an ethical space of encounter, respect, negotiation and collaboration without the dominance or judgement of distant and enveloping authority'.[21] The declaration includes five priority areas for immediate action, with the fifth focussing specifically on support for Indigenous self-determination in alignment with the principles articulated in the UNDRIP.[22] The priority areas are summarised as follows:

1) Knowledge Authorities – Calls for acknowledgement of Indigenous knowledge frameworks and the need for archives to engage in reciprocal and respectful relationships to weave Indigenous worldviews into institutional collections to decolonise state-sanctioned memories.
2) Property and Ownership – Understanding and recognising Indigenous ownership of Indigenous traditional knowledge, cultural expression, knowledge and intellectual property.
3) Recognition and Identity – Understanding internationally the long histories of colonisation that have impacted Indigenous people's struggle for recognition. Urging the archives to recognise Indigenous people across archival systems as holding unique kinship, identity and cultures as distinct peoples. Expresses the need for participatory descriptive practices and recognition of Indigenous knowledges as living and connected to place.
4) Research and Access – Recognises the tensions between European and Indigenous ways of knowing. Stresses the importance of Indigenous control over access to information in colonial archives, changes to recordkeeping legislation and practice to incorporate IDS, a right of reply and redress.
5) Self-Determination – Recognises the principles of the UNDRIP as forming the basis of the declaration in an archival context.[23]

While limited information is available on the implementation of the declaration, there is no doubt that it has served as an important tool for raising awareness of Indigenous priorities in the sector. In an Australian context, the declaration has been promoted across archival institutions and associations, including, for example, being referenced as a key guiding document by the National Archives of Australia in their submission made for REVIVE, *The National Cultural Policy*[24]; endorsed by the National and State Libraries of Australasia (NSLA); and referred to as a guiding document by AIATSIS (Australian Institute of Aboriginal and Torres Strait Islander Studies) and the Council of Australasian Archives and Records Authorities (CAARA).[25] More broadly, it has been debated and discussed in scholarly research in Australia,[26] helping to generate discussion about the importance of greater reporting on the implementation of the declaration for understanding how it is being utilised in practice.[27] Nationally, the declaration has brought hope that a refiguring of archival practices can take place to support Indigenous self-determination. Like UNDRIP, there is recognition that the declaration can guide peak bodies and professional associations to articulate social justice commitments. This advocacy, in turn, influences organisational approaches and practices across GLAM institutions.

Ensuring Indigenous self-determination is embedded in the activation of declarations and frameworks

The declaration and associated statements of support have been designed to support significant transformations of Indigenous archiving approaches, and this requires that principles of Indigenous self-determination are built into all implementation and review processes. Indigenous governance and decision-making are critical. The international IDS movement provides a pathway for Indigenous self-determination to be built into the activation of declarations and frameworks. Broadly, the IDS movement empowers Indigenous people to exercise rights of ownership and control over data to inform self-determined priorities and goals. The rise of the IDS and Indigenous Data Governance (IDG) movement highlights the growing trend towards Indigenous-led ethical approaches to data collection and management across a range of disciplines and sectors. As a global endeavour, the application of IDS principles in Indigenous community contexts is an emerging area of research exploring a range of concerns, from legal and ethical dimensions around data storage, ownership, access and consent to intellectual property rights and practical considerations about how data are used in the context of research, policy and practice.[28] The leading international *Care Principles of Indigenous Data Governance* (CARE), which focus on self-determination and Indigenous innovation, and the national Maiam Nayri Wingara *Indigenous Data Sovereignty Communique* are roadmaps for embedding Indigenous governance to support self-determination.[29] They assert Indigenous-led data management practices and approaches to ensure respect for Indigenous decision making.

The archives sector must consider IDS and IDG principles in national and international declarations and frameworks. It is also critical that we identify and address tensions related to the strategic approaches that the declaration and frameworks articulate, particularly in understanding if the priorities are focused on institutional archives and their needs rather than local community needs.[30] The success of the declarations relies on institutional archives working meaningfully with Indigenous people and communities to support their aspirations for archival self-determination. An institution needs strategy to support Indigenous engagement otherwise the work risks being ad hoc and reactive. This is of particular concern where governance structures are not put in place to support First Nations decision-making in archival practice. It can result in continued tensions and distrust between First Nations communities and institutional archives. Open communication and transparency must be developed to support two-way engagement between the archives and communities. To improve the implementation and realisation of the goals expressed in professional declarations, we must bridge gaps between research and practice. To bring the statements to life and indeed activate them through principles of Indigenous self-determination, we need to be transparent about the methods and approaches for their implementation. Greater accountability on Indigenous participation, aligned with IDS and IDG principles, is required for the statements to be more than merely symbolic gestures without tangible measures for changing practice.

Designing research to support first nations self-determination in the archives
In this section, I turn to my own research to discuss the role that Indigenous research methodologies and research methods could play in developing a focused agenda for change in line with the aspirations found in professional declarations and statements.

In 2019, I wrote about my personal journey of professional practice in supporting Indigenous priorities and self-determination in Australian libraries and archives. At a time when I decided that I would make a sharp turn to academic research, I discussed the need for the sector to engage in more rigorous and difficult dialogue about the complex and contested nature of the archives for First Nations people. I stressed the importance of Indigenous research methodologies being developed and applied to support a transformation of libraries and archives aligned with Indigenous ways of knowing, being and doing. It was a call to action for libraries and archives to increase the use of Indigenous research methodologies – across both research and practice – to seek ways to decolonise and simultaneously indigenise the archives.[31] In the article, I discussed areas of tension and gaps that needed addressing including:

- A lack of critical dialogue about First Nations self-determination and cultural safety.
- The existence of poor project design, which although developed with good intention, ignored deep structural issues and power dynamics related to the contested nature of the archives.
- A lack of projects co-designed with First Nations community input and lack of acknowledgement and incorporation of community priorities and desires.
- Repeated decadal conversations around the same complex problems.

Four years after the article was published, I feel empowered by the opportunities that have arisen from bridging the gap between research and practice. Being engaged in developing critical participatory research projects has helped me to develop an evidence base for advancing Indigenous self-determined priorities across library and archival practice. I am aware of the importance and impact of redirecting my labour to work with communities to explore the application of Indigenous methodologies and frameworks in reimagining Indigenous archival futures. In my view, archival practice can only change with a commitment to research. While I recognise the importance of professional statements for action, I am also aware that a lack of focus can lead them to be performative tools that move the sector no further than mere symbolism.

To demonstrate the use of an Indigenous research paradigm, I further describe research undertaken as part of my doctoral project *Unclasping the White Hand: Reclaiming and Refiguring the Archives to Support Indigenous Wellbeing and Sovereignty*. I do this to provide a clear example of how research can enable an in-depth analysis of questions related to Indigenous self-determination in the archives. Broadly, the doctoral research explored whether the current dominant approaches to archiving and managing Aboriginal and Torres Strait Islander knowledges support the wellbeing of Indigenous people and recognise Indigenous sovereignty in an archival context. It investigated the contested nature of the archives and the level of agency that Indigenous people have to control and own their archives. The research, framed in an Indigenous research paradigm, helped build cyclical and reflexive research grounded in supporting reciprocity and respect in research relationships.

Relational research and Indigenous research paradigms
Linda Tuhiwai Smith (2021), who led critical conversations internationally about the need to decolonise Indigenous research, outlined the history of distrust within research *about* Indigenous people and the need for a new agenda to support Indigenous self-determination in research.[32] An Indigenous research paradigm establishes a pathway for building this trust to work towards the goal of self-determination. According to Shawn Wilson, an Indigenous research paradigm is guided fundamentally by the belief that knowledge is relational. It is a research paradigm that rejects the view of knowledge being held by an individual or something that can be gained.

> You are not just gaining information from people; you are sharing your information. You are analysing and you are building ideas and relationships as well. Research is not just something that's out there: it's something that you're building for yourself and for your community.[33]

Wilson's articulation of an Indigenous research paradigm gave me a sense-making tool. It helped me consider my research within an Indigenous research paradigm based on the four key elements of ontology, epistemology, methodology and axiology. Wilson explains that ontologies (the belief in the nature of our reality) and our epistemologies (the way we think about that reality) connect with research methodologies as a way of gaining and building more knowledge about our own specific realities. He describes a research paradigm as being informed by these ontological and epistemological positions and our own judgments about values, ethics or axiology. The four elements are not considered linear or bound by time but flow and connect in a circular and interrelated way.[34] I situated the research firmly within an Indigenous research paradigm to give depth, insight and accountability to the questions I was investigating in a way that acknowledged the relationality of the research. Importantly, I could not shy away from the fact that I was deeply related to the research questions, not just on an intellectual level but also in mind, body and spirit.

Early in the research design stage of my doctoral studies, I found myself laying out a tangled web of what I saw as the significant research problems about the relationships of Indigenous people with libraries and archives. I entered my doctorate with the purposeful aim of designing research that would give back to First Nations people and communities in Australia. I also wanted to contribute to scholarship in library, archival and Indigenous studies with a view to transformation, as I was very aware of the critical lack of research in the field. It was also vital that I considered the four principles set out in *The AIATSIS Code* 2020, namely, to support (1) Indigenous self-determination, (2) Indigenous leadership, (3) Impact and value and (4) Sustainability and accountability.[35] Through a series of yarning sessions and the use of autoethnography, the research design enabled an ethical framework to examine the holistic needs of Indigenous people in the archives to support Indigenous archiving and memory keeping and the need to repair and seek justice from the impacts of colonisation.

I selected methods congruent with Indigenous worldviews and the Indigenous research paradigm.[36] Wilson (2001) provided useful questions to evaluate the appropriateness of research methods, including:

What is my role as researcher, and what are my obligations?
Does this method allow me to fulfil my obligations in my role?
Does this method help to build a relationship between myself as a researcher and my research topic?
Does it build respectful relationships with the other participants in the research?[37]

I utilised data collection and analysis methods that explicitly addressed the research questions, drawing in data on my personal and professional experiences and engagement with research participants. The suitability of the research design enabled me to engage with the stories of First Nations people and allies who were engaging with the archives in Australia.

Within the research I undertook a series of 15 yarning sessions with participants covering four cohort groups including Indigenous people from the GLAM sector; Indigenous scholars who have researched or engaged with libraries and archives; Indigenous Elders who have knowledge and or experiences of libraries and archives and Advocates for Indigenous priorities (non-Indigenous professionals and workers) who are allies in the sector. Research participants were recruited to contribute insights to the study based on their previous experience and knowledge of the area. I used autoethnography to reflect deeply on my own professional experiences working as an archivist to support Indigenous engagement and the development of protocols and policy across library and archive settings. The research identified immediate reforms required to support Indigenous people's archiving needs and outlined a transformative model of Indigenous Living Archives on Country to support Indigenous ways of knowing, being and doing in the archives and redress for the impacts of colonisation.

Applying Indigenous research methodologies and methods

Here I will describe how the research drew on Indigenous standpoint theory, Yarning methodologies and Indigenous Storywork within a critical theory framework to consider the engagement of First Nations people with the archives.[38] I also outline the data collection and analysis methods utilised to support these Indigenous research methodologies, and highlight how each methodology and method supported respectful and reciprocal engagement within the research.

Indigenous standpoint theory

Indigenous standpoint enables opportunities for researchers to understand more about their place in the world and how that position determines *what we do* and *what we don't know*. Within academic research, marginalised groups have utilised standpoint theory as a method of inquiry to raise the voice of those people whose accounts or experiences were previously excluded or subjugated within intellectual knowledge production.[39] Behrendt's description of Indigenous standpoint outlines that 'your positioning or your standpoint – will fundamentally influence the way you see the world. Indigenous standpoint notes up front that we, as individuals, are shaped by our cultures, cultural values, and experiences with society's institutions'.[40]

I had pre-existing relationships with the research topic, and these experiences influenced my research approach. My employment experiences and engagement in professional practice provided a significant backdrop to the study and my standpoint in the research. My experiences developing policy, protocols, practice and spaces for Indigenous people to have agency in libraries and archives situated how I knew and understood the research topic, and my knowledge through these professional and lived experiences and interactions could not be ignored. Due to my experiences, I also had insider positionality, meaning that I was an insider researcher. This provided a closeness to the research topic and questions, which meant the research was deeply subjective. Merriam and colleagues (2001) explain the challenges associated with questions of power and positionality within insider and outsider researcher roles. The authors discuss questions and complexities related to researching class, gender and culture and note that the framing of insider and outsider research allows for people to understand power dynamics when researching within and across one's own culture.[41] Similarly, Fredericks discusses insider research focusing on researching Indigenous women, as an Indigenous woman. Fredericks notes that the skills that are required to negotiate this positionality are that 'Indigenous researchers work within a set of "insider" dynamics, and it takes considerable sensitivity, skills, maturity, experience and knowledge to work these issues through'.[42]

I used autoethnographic methods within the research, specifically from the literature on Indigenous Autoethnography, to reflect on my own professional experiences through a process of journaling and reflection.[43] It became a critical tool for me to draw out issues that had emerged over my professional career on both an 'experiential and intellectual level'.[44] Utilising these Indigenous methodologies and methods helped me to occupy the position of an insider researcher clearly and transparently. Overall, it required me to be a reflexive researcher and to practice reciprocity in the research thoughtfully and respectfully.

Yarning methodologies

> Yarning is our way. The narrative way is always the way we have done stuff, so it is the best way. It is the cultural way. It is the safe way. (Aunty Glendra Stubbs)[45]

Yarning is a vital methodology to build trust and an open and respectful space for engaging in Indigenous research topics. In my case, I used yarning as a tool to discuss Indigenous wellbeing and sovereignty in the archives. Initially, I considered yarning as a vital data-collection method. However, as the research progressed, yarning became a critical participatory methodology to guide the overall research engagement. The yarning approach aligned with Wilson's earlier articulation of relational research. The use of yarning in research is not only about building relational accountability with the living but also about caring for and respecting Country and Ancestors who are a part of the research stories. I connect deeply with a description provided by Barlo and colleagues (2021) as follows:

> Yarning is a powerful methodology from the vantage point of a relationship journey because the process engages the researcher in a web of relationships which includes research participants, the knowledges and stories themselves, Ancestors and Country, and histories and futures as they live in the telling and hearing of stories.[46]

Bessarab and Ng'andu described how, as a research method, yarning is used to learn a person's story or to find out more about their knowledge and experiences.[47] Other scholars have described the importance of yarning as a culturally safe method of data collection and a tool for building partnerships in the research process. It is a way to build strength around Indigenous voice and participation, particularly with 'knowledge systems, ways of doing, perspectives and participation in research'.[48] Fredericks and colleagues (2011) describe yarning as an action research method and a tool for empowerment to work with Indigenous Australian people as it allows for 'a relaxed and familiar communication process'.[49] Adams and Faulkhead similarly describe yarning as a narrative research method that involves self-reflection and deep discussion about a particular issue and which involves exploring similar or different ideas in explaining concepts, leading to new information and understandings.[50]

I found that yarning aligned with the focus of my research being about relationships as it suited these participatory approaches. I considered that the research participants were partners in the research, and yarning helped facilitate a process for ongoing dialogue and rigour around the accountability of the data and stories used in the research. On a practical level, it meant that my research relationships extended beyond the data-collection phase through data analysis and then finally built feedback into the overall use of material in the research write-up. I sought consent for the use of any quotes or material that was from the direct voice of participants. I built into my ethics process the ability to provide full attribution of people's knowledge and experience in any written content.

Indigenous storywork

> Story is a way forward in the decolonizing movement as deep meaning-making encounter, as expansive creative collaboration.[51]

Indigenous Storywork is considered both a methodology and a method that supports Indigenous storytelling and the transmission of knowledge through orality.[52] Archibald describes the power of knowledge transmission and the important role of collecting and sharing that knowledge through respectful processes. 'The storyteller's responsibility toward others is linked to the power that her/his stories may have'.[53] There are seven elements to Archibald's (2008) Indigenous Storywork principles: (1) respect, (2) responsibility, (3) reciprocity, (4) reverence, (5) holism, (6) interrelatedness, and (7) synergy. Broadly, the principles remind us about the importance of holism and that when acquiring new knowledge, like being involved in research, these practices continue to be linked to cultural practices.[54] Drawing on the Storywork methodology, De Santolo described how Indigenous storytelling is a decolonising research approach, enabling possibilities for transformational resistance through a research approach grounded in relationships.[55]

In my research, Indigenous Storywork allowed a conversational method to come into play throughout the research process. It was also strongly aligned as an approach to support the connection in the research with Indigenous standpoint theory. Archibald's principles were guiding principles used throughout the research to listen to, read, interpret and consider the research stories. I contextualised the autoethnographic and yarning approaches in the broader view of Indigenous Storywork as a method to intertwine the voice and stories of other research participants within my own research insights. It enabled the voices and stories of my own lived experiences and other Indigenous participants to be combined within the research. Putting my stories and others together was a powerful process that spotlighted peoples' resilience and determination to support better approaches to Indigenous archiving and engagement with collections.

The effectiveness of Indigenous research methods in meeting the goals of the research

The Indigenous research methodologies and methods outlined earlier in the text enabled a respectful research approach to delve deep into questions about Indigenous-led approaches to archiving and memory-keeping in an Indigenous context in Australia. Trust and reciprocity were crucial elements of the research design process, as the yarning sessions opened a space for the respectful sharing of stories. Participants understood that the information they shared would be considered deeply beyond a transactional approach and that, from the data collection stage, there was a commitment to share and validate research findings through continued yarning. Building a trusted space for discussion and by centring Indigenous ways of knowing, being and doing, the research privileged First Nations research priorities. In addition, this required that the design responded to colonial legacies of distrust in research.

Being aware of this impact of colonisation was critical, and particularly to understand the relationships between First Nations people and archival institutions.

Indigenous research methodologies are critical tools for archives to support Indigenous self-determination. The research findings identified that the use of Indigenous research methodologies was effective and they could support disruption and change within the sector. They also demonstrated the importance of embedding Indigenous research ethics in studies. In particular, the principles of respect, trust and reciprocity were essential to support the telling of stories. The research design was empowering, and it privileged Indigenous voices and representation. The relationship between research and practice was evident in the research project. Both the autoethnography and the yarning sessions provided significant insight into ways in which the archives are contested for First Nations people. The major findings of my doctoral studies directly relate to action required in archival practice. This clearly demonstrates the importance of the research and practice relationship.

First, the *Critique of the term cultural safety as insufficient to support Indigenous people in an archival context* identified the problematic nature of the term 'cultural safety' in an archival context. While the term was originally utilised to discuss the topics relating to Indigenous people's calls for greater control of the archives, the research identified that the term was insufficient to encapsulate First Nations people's needs. The definition in an archival context lacks attention to the systemic and structural issues that resulted from the ongoing colonisation of Australia. In particular, it oversimplifies the complex and multifaceted requirements needed to support an effective critique of the tools of colonisation as they are manifested in the archives and institutions of Australian society. These findings are vital for archival institutions to understand if they are to build appropriate responses for the training and education of staff.

Secondly, the research identified new approaches for understanding Indigenous wellbeing in the archives more compatible with Indigenous ways of knowing, being and doing that could also communicate the broad needs of First Nations people in the archives beyond the term cultural safety. These new approaches are described in a working definition of *Indigenous wellbeing, sovereignty and archival sovereignty*. The definition enables a view of what a healthy and safe archive looks like for First Nations people and as such is a benchmark for archives to consider whether in co-designing services for communities, or building greater engagement and decision-making over the control and use of data from communities. The working definition is future focused and shines a light on the important work that the archives can be involved with to support Indigenous people's social, emotional and cultural wellbeing in the archives.

Next, the research findings included an *In-depth analysis of the harmful impacts on Indigenous wellbeing and sovereignty of the colonial archival model and approaches* by listing the current challenges that exist within the archives. The research stories provided detailed descriptions of the immediate harms and dangers that exist to Indigenous people's social and emotional wellbeing. These harms and dangers are critical for archival institutions to understand to mitigate risks within their organisational policies and procedures.

The final two research findings provide pathways for immediate reforms of the archives and transformations that are required in the long-term to support Indigenous self-determination and priorities by keeping archives locally connected to community, and on Country. The *Indigenous Archiving Reforms* include six key areas: (1) Indigenous Protocols to support Indigenous wellbeing, sovereignty and archival sovereignty; (2) Recognising the archives as a place of Sorry Business; (3) Indigenous stewardship and custodianship of materials held in the archives; (4) Indigenous cultural practices and ceremonies in the archives; (5) Returning love to ancestors who are captured in the archives and (6) IDS and the archives. Finally, a *Transformative Model of Indigenous Living Archives on Country* was proposed. The core features identified in the model include support for: Indigenous wellbeing and archival sovereignty holistically embedded in the archives; Indigenous knowledge management protocols in the archives, that are locally defined, and place based, and that incorporate spiritual and emotional needs and Indigenous archival sovereignty recognised through transparent local decision-making.

Discussion and reflections

The Indigenous-led research methodologies and methods discussed here provide an example of how research can support an agenda of disruption and change for Indigenous priorities in the archives. The findings demonstrate the layers of information exchange that took place in the research. Earlier in the paper I described how national and international professional declarations and statements of support set pathways for increasing Indigenous engagement with the archives. However, while recognising the importance of these as tools for change, I also signalled the vital need for greater transparency about Indigenous participation in decision-making in bringing the statements to life, notably by including principles articulated in the IDS and IDG movement. The Indigenous research methodologies and methods of Yarning, Indigenous Standpoint and Indigenous Storywork illustrate how research can help build the relationships required to support this.

Because of the nature of their international, national or state-based approaches, archival declarations and statements homogenise First Nations priorities rather than recognising communities as diverse groups with diverse and locally situated needs. These statements and principles aim to support First Nations priorities; however, to date, they have been developed in professional and institutional contexts rather than making the direct voice of First Nations people and their community needs visible. Indigenous research methodologies seek to engage Indigenous people through yarning and hearing people's stories, which supports the recognition of their unique standpoint. Combined, the methodologies open space for reciprocal relationships for deep listening to take place and for trust to be built. Developing an ethical foundation of exchange enables opportunities for archival institutions to find solutions for addressing complex and systemic issues with more rigour. The methodologies and methods provide an approach for relational accountability and transparency on what questions are being asked and who is participating in dialogue about the research questions. An Indigenous self-determination agenda is further realised by shifting the focus from institutional agendas to balance Indigenous-led community-driven priorities.

At the minimum, archival practice should be guided by principles of Indigenous self-determination articulated across the UNDRIP, the AIATSIS Research Code and the Tandanya-Adelaide declaration. Any projects that include First Nations cultural heritage should include representation of Indigenous people. This representation must focus on co-design and participation in decision-making to ensure that First Nations people's interests are understood in a governance context. Returning to the examples of the ASA *Policy Statement on Archival Services and Aboriginal and Torres Strait Islander Peoples* and the ICA's *Tandanya Adelaide Declaration*, it is evident that Indigenous research methodologies and approaches would be beneficial tools for implementing action to support their agendas. In the case of any upcoming reviews of the declarations and statements there is a case for the profession to consider IDS and IDG principles within the activation of the statements. The assertion of rights outlined in the growing IDS movement requires that archives engage deeply with locally defined Indigenous priorities. In the future, more scrutiny will be placed on institutions to be accountable for their support for IDG and decision-making. Applying Indigenous Research Methodologies further enhances this work to bring transparency to the fore.

Pathways to strengthen the research and practice relationships for Indigenous archives

It is an exciting prospect that archivists and information workers in Australia and internationally increase their understanding and literacy of Indigenous research methodologies and approaches to build respect and reciprocal accountability in projects. Indigenous research methodologies bring transparency to projects and further opportunities for rigour in defining and answering questions that need examining. The articulation of declarations and statements demonstrates the goodwill of the archives sector in increasing support for Indigenous engagement. However, there are significant opportunities for embedding more grounded approaches that bring mutual benefits to both institutions and communities.

The Indigenous research methodologies of Yarning, Indigenous Standpoint and Indigenous Storywork are approaches that can support archivists and information workers in responding to community needs within practice. The archives profession must avoid approaching complex questions with band-aid solutions. This paper has encouraged more significant support for archivists to engage in reflexive practice guided by Indigenous research methodologies and methods. Open and transparent planning around research and projects can support the building of trust to surface areas of action required for Indigenous self-determination in the archives. They also help break down barriers and guide robust dialogue across institutional and community contexts.

Acknowledgements

The author acknowledges the traditional owners of the various First Nations lands where this research was conducted, and pay my respect to Elders, past and present. The author also acknowledge the research participants who contributed their stories and experiences in the doctoral studies and is deeply thankful their your time, input and expertise. The author also thanks the supervisors of her doctoral studies Professor Sue McKemmish, Dr Alex Byrne and Dr Shannon Faulkhead and also the editors of the journal and is thankful for the comments received in the peer review. The more she writes, the more she realises realise the importance of the community of practice that exists around her. She appreciates their time and comments to sharpen and make improvements to the article.

Conflict of interests and funding

This research was supported by an Australian Government Research Training Program (RTP) Scholarship. No potential conflict of interest was reported by the author.

Notes on the contributor

Dr Kirsten Thorpe (Worimi, Port Stephens), Associate Professor, is a Chancellor's Indigenous Research Fellow at the Jumbunna Institute for Indigenous Education & Research, University of Technology Sydney (UTS). Kirsten leads the Indigenous Archives and Data Stewardship Hub, which advocates for Indigenous rights in archives and data, and develops research and engagement in relation to refiguring libraries and archives to support the culturally appropriate ownership, management and ongoing preservation of Indigenous knowledges. Kirsten has broad interests in research and engagement with Indigenous protocols and decolonising practices in the library and archive fields, and the broader GLAM (Galleries, Libraries, Archives and Museums) sector. Kirsten advocates for the 'right of reply' to records, and capacity building and support for the development of Living Indigenous Archives on Country. Kirsten is an invited member of the ICA Expert Group on Indigenous Matters, an elected member of the International Federation of Library Associations and Institutions (IFLA) Indigenous Matters Standing Committee, and a co-founder of the Indigenous Archives Collective.

ORCID

Kirsten Thorpe

Notes

1. Kirsten Thorpe, 'Unclasping the White Hand: Reclaiming and Refiguring the Archives to Support Indigenous Wellbeing and Sovereignty', PhD Thesis, Monash University, 2022, p. 169.
2. Australian Society of Archivists (ASA), Policy Statement on Archival Services and Aboriginal and Torres Strait Islander Peoples, 1996, available at https://www.archivists.org.au/documents/item/32#:~:text=Archives%20have%20the%20opportunity%20and,cultural%20heritage%20and%20historical%20experience, accessed 1 November 2023; International Council on Archives (ICA), Tandanya – Adelaide Declaration, available at https://www.naa.gov.au/sites/default/files/2020-06/Tandanya-Adelaide-Declaration.pdf, accessed 29 October 2023.
3. Thorpe, 'Unclasping the White Hand'.
4. Henrietta Fourmile, 'Who Owns the Past?: Aborigines as Captives of the Archives', Aboriginal History, vol. 13, no. 1–2, 1989, pp. 1–9; see also Faulkhead Shannon, et al., 'Australian Indigenous Knowledge and the Archives: Embracing Multiple Ways of Knowing and Keeping', Archives and Manuscripts, vol. 38, no. 1, 2010, pp. 27–50.
5. See for example: Lynette Russell, A Little Bird Told Me: Family Secrets, Necessary Lies, Allen & Unwin, Crows Nest, NSW, 2002; Genevieve Grieves and Odette Kelada, 'Bleeding the Archive, Transforming the Mythscape', in I. McLean and D. Jorgensen (eds.), Indigenous Archives The Making and Unmaking of Aboriginal Art, vol. 1, UWA Press, Crawley, Western Australia, 2017, pp. 321–41; and Loris Williams, Andrew Wilson, and Author, 'Identity and Access to Government Records: Empowering the Community [Archives relating to Aboriginal people.]' Archives and Manuscripts, vol 34, no. 1, 2006, pp. 8–30.
6. Henrietta Fourmile, 'Who Owns the Past?: Aborigines as Captives of the Archives', Aboriginal History, vol. 13, no. 1–2 (1989), pp. 1–9; see also Shannon, Faulkhead, et al., 'Australian Indigenous Knowledge and the Archives: Embracing Multiple Ways of Knowing and Keeping', Archives and Manuscripts, vol. 38, no. 1, 2010, pp. 27–50.
7. Thorpe, 'Unclasping the White Hand'.
8. Terri Janke, True Tracks: Respecting Indigenous Knowledge and Culture, New South Wales University Press, Sydney, NSW, 2021.
9. Natalie Harkin, 'The Poetics of (Re) mapping Archives: Memory in the Blood', Journal of the Association for the Study of Australian Literature, vol. 14, no. 3, 2014, pp. 1–14.
10. Martin Nakata, Vicky Nakata, Alex Byrne, Gabrielle Gardiner, 'Indigenous Knowledge, the Library and Information Service Sector, and Protocols', Australian Academic & Research Libraries, vol. 36, no. 2, 2005, pp. 7–21.
11. Aboriginal and Torres Strait Islander Library, Information and Resource Network (ATSILIRN) 'Protocols for Libraries, Archives and Information Services', available at https://atsilirn.aiatsis.gov.au/protocols.php, accessed 25 October 2023.
12. Australian Society of Archivists (ASA), Policy Statement on Archival Services and Aboriginal and Torres Strait Islander Peoples.
13. Allison Boucher Krebs, 'Native America's Twenty-first-Century Right to Know', Archival Science, vol. 12, 2012, pp. 173–190. https://doi.org/10.1007/s10502-011-9161-2
14. Jennifer R. O'Neal, '"The Right to Know": Decolonizing Native American Archives', Journal of Western Archives, vol 6, no. 1, 2015, available at http://hdl.handle.net/1794/19360
15. Raymond O. Frogner, 'The Train from Dunvegan: Implementing the United Nations Declaration on the Rights of Indigenous Peoples (UNDRIP) in Public Archives in Canada', Archival Science, vol. 22, no. 2, 2022, pp. 209–38.
16. The body of scholarship relating to Indigenous librarianship is vital to consider in relation to the movement to consider calls for action for Indigenous archives. Recognising that a key concept for both the library, information and archiving fields is the care, protection and appropriate stewardship of Indigenous knowledges. For a recent overview of the movement see: Ulia Gosart, 'Indigenous Librarianship: Theory, Practices, and Means of Social Action', IFLA Journal, vol. 47, no. 3, 2021, pp. 293–304.
17. Amy Griffin, International Indigenous Librarians' Forum (IILF) guide, 2023, available at: https://trw.org.nz/professional-development/iilf-international-indigenous-librarians-forum/, accessed 29 February 2024.
18. The history of the development of the Protocols for Native American Archival Materials, including key readings and research is available on the Society of American Archivists website at: https://www2.archivists.org/groups/native-american-archives-section/protocols-for-native-american-archival-materials-information-and-resources-page

19. Association of Canadian Archivists, Truth and Reconciliation, available at https://archivists.ca/Truth-and-Reconciliation, accessed 20 February 2024.
20. Truth and Reconciliation Commission of Canada, Truth and Reconciliation Commission of Canada: Calls to Action, 2015, available at https://archives2026.files.wordpress.com/2022/02/reconciliationframeworkreport_en.pdf, accessed 1 March 2024.
21. International Council on Archives, Tandanya-Adelaide Declaration, 2019, p. 2, available at https://www.naa.gov.au/sites/default/files/2020-06/Tandanya-Adelaide-Declaration.pdf, accessed 20 October 2023.
22. United Nations, United Nations Declaration on the Rights of Indigenous Peoples, 2007, available at https://www.un.org/development/desa/indigenouspeoples/wp-content/uploads/sites/19/2018/11/UNDRIP_E_web.pdf, accessed 5 November 2023.
23. International Council on Archives, Tandanya-Adelaide Declaration, pp. 3–4.
24. https://www.arts.gov.au/sites/default/files/documents/a-new-national-cultural-policy-ncp0848-national-archives-of-australia.pdf
25. https://www.nsla.org.au/resources/tandanya-declaration/; https://aiatsis.gov.au/tandanya-declaration; https://www.caara.org.au/index.php/news/
26. See for example Barrowcliffe Rose, et al. 'Activating and Supporting the Tandanya Adelaide Declaration on Indigenous Archives', Archives and Manuscripts, vol. 49, no. 3, 2021, pp. 167–85; Indigenous Archives Collective, 'The Indigenous Archives Collective Position Statement on the Right of Reply to Indigenous Knowledges and Information Held in Archives', Archives and Manuscripts, vol. 49, no. 3, 2021, pp. 244–52; Linda Barwick, et al. 'Reclaiming Archives: Guest Editorial', Preservation, Digital Technology & Culture, vol 50, no. 3–4, 2021, pp. 99–104; Anja Schwarz, Fiona Möhrle and Sabine von Mering. 'Collections from Colonial Australia in Berlin's Museum für Naturkunde and the Challenges of Data Accessibility', Biodiversity Information Science and Standards, vol. 7, 2023, e111980.
27. For example, a panel *Tandanya: Becoming* at the 2022 Australian Institute for Aboriginal and Torres Strait Islander Studies (AIATSIS) Summit in 2022. Australian Institute for Aboriginal and Torres Strait Islander Studies (AIATSIS) '2022 AIATSIS Summit', Program: https://aiatsis.gov.au/sites/default/files/2022-06/2022-aiatsis-summit-program-16-june.pdf
28. Tahu Kukutai and John Taylor, Indigenous Data Sovereignty: Toward an Agenda, ANU Press, Acton, ACT, 2016.
29. Global Indigenous Data Alliance (GIDA), CARE Principles for Indigenous Data Governance, GIDA, 2019, available at https://www.gida-global.org/care; Maiam Nayri Wingara & Australian Indigenous Governance Institute, Key Principles, 2018, available at https://www.maiamnayriwingara.org/mnw-principles, accessed 21 October 2024.
30. Barrowcliffe et al., 'Activating and Supporting the Tandanya Adelaide Declaration on Indigenous Archives', pp. 167–85.
31. Kirsten Thorpe, 'Transformative Praxis-Building Spaces for Indigenous Self-determination in Libraries and Archives', *In the Library with the Lead Pipe*, 2019, available at https://www.inthelibrarywiththeleadpipe.org/2019/transformative-praxis/, accessed 31 May 2024.
32. Linda Tuhiwai Smith, Decolonizing Methodologies: Research and Indigenous Peoples, Bloomsbury Publishing, London, 2021.
33. Shawn Wilson, 'What Is an Indigenous Research Methodology?', Canadian Journal of Native Education, vol. 25, no. 2, 2001, p. 179.
34. Shawn Wilson, Research Is Ceremony. Indigenous Research Methods, Fernwood, Winnipeg, 2008, p. 70.
35. Australian Institute for Aboriginal and Torres Strait Islander Studies (AIATSIS), Code of Ethics for Aboriginal and Torres Strait Islander Research, 2020, available at https://aiatsis.gov.au/sites/default/files/2020-10/aiatsis-code-ethics.pdf, accessed 1 November 2023.
36. Margaret Kovach, 'Conversational Method in Indigenous Research', First Peoples Child & Family Review, vol. 14, no. 1, 2010, p. 40.
37. Shawn Wilson, 'What is an Indigenous Research Methodology?', Canadian Journal of Native Education, vol. 25, no. 2, 2001, p. 178.
38. Dennis Foley, 'Indigenous Epistemology and Indigenous Standpoint Theory', Social Alternatives, vol. 22, no. 1, 2003, p. 44; Martin Nakata, Disciplining the Savages: Savaging the Disciplines, Aboriginal Studies Press, Canberra ACT, 2007, pp. 195–212; Sue McKemmish, 'Placing Records Continuum Theory and Practice', Archival Science, vol. 1, no. 4, 2001, pp. 333–59; Joanne A. Archibald, Indigenous Storywork: Educating the Heart, Mind, Body, and spirit, UBC Press, Vancouver, 2008; Petah Atkinson, Marilyn Baird, and Karen Adams, 'Are You Really Using Yarning Research? Mapping Social and Family

38. Yarning to Strengthen Yarning Research Quality', AlterNative: An International Journal of Indigenous Peoples, vol. 17, no. 2, 2021, pp. 191–201.
39. Martin Nakata, Disciplining the Savages, pp. 195–212.
40. Larissa Behrendt, 'Indigenous Story-telling: Decolonising Institutions and Assertive Self-determination and Implications for Legal Practice', Decolonizing Research Indigenous Storywork As Methodology, 2019, pp. 175–186.
41. Sharan Merriam, et al., 'Power and Positionality: Negotiating Insider/Outsider Status Within and Across Cultures', International Journal of Lifelong Education, vol. 20, no. 5, 2001, p. 405.
42. Linda Smith 1999, cited in Bronwyn Fredericks, 'Researching with Aboriginal Women as an Aboriginal Woman Researcher', Australian Feminist Studies, vol. 23, no. 55, 1999, p. 120.
43. Jennifer Houston, 'Indigenous Autoethnography: Formulating Our Knowledge, Our Way', The Australian Journal of Indigenous Education, vol. 36, Suppl. 1, 2007, pp. 45–50.
44. Roxanne Bainbridge, 'Autoethnography in Indigenous Research Contexts: The Value of Inner Knowing', Journal of Australian Indigenous Issues, vol 10, no. 2, 2007, pp. 54–64.
45. Thorpe, 'Unclasping the White Hand', p. 125.
46. Stuart Barlo, et al., 'Yarning as Protected Space: Relational Accountability in Research', AlterNative: An International Journal of Indigenous Peoples, vol. 17, no. 1, 2021, p. 46.
47. Dawn Bessarab and Bridget Ng'Andu, 'Yarning About Yarning as a Legitimate Method in Indigenous Research', International Journal of Critical Indigenous Studies, vol. 3, no. 1, 2010, p. 38, pp. 37–50.
48. Cheree Dean, 'A Yarning Place in Narrative Histories', History of Education Review, vol. 39, no. 2, 2010, p. 10.
49. Bronwyn Fredericks, et al., 'Engaging the Practice of Indigenous Yarning in Action Research', ALAR: Action Learning and Action Research Journal, vol. 17, no. 2, 2011, p. 8; Petah Atkinson, Marilyn Baird, and Karen Adams, 'Are You Really Using Yarning Research? Mapping Social and Family Yarning to Strengthen Yarning Research Quality', AlterNative: An International Journal of Indigenous Peoples, vol. 17, no. 2, 2021, pp. 191–201.
50. Karen Adams and Shannon Faulkhead, 'This Is Not a Guide to Indigenous Research Partnerships: But It Could Help', Information, Communication & Society, vol. 15, no. 7, 2012, p. 4.
51. Jason De Santolo, 'Indigenous Storywork in Australia', in Jo-Ann Archibald Q'um Q'um Xiiem, et al. (eds.), Decolonizing Research: Indigenous Storywork As Methodology, Bloomsbury Academic & Professional, London, 2019, p. 171.
52. Joanne A. Archibald, Indigenous Storywork: Educating the Heart, Mind, Body, and Spirit, UBC Press, 2008.
53. Ibid. p. 27.
54. Ibid, p. 11.
55. De Santolo, 'Indigenous Storywork in Australia', p. 172.

ARTICLE

The Challenge of Actualising Research in Practice: Implementing the Charter of Lifelong Rights in Childhood Recordkeeping in Out of Home Care

Frank Golding[1], Sue McKemmish[2] and Barbara Reed[3]

[1]Care Leavers Australasia Network (CLAN) and Federation University, Melbourne, Australia;
[2]Monash University, Melbourne, Australia; [3]Monash University, Melbourne, Australia

Abstract

This paper addresses the challenges encountered when actualising research in practice, using the implementation of the Charter of Lifelong Rights in Childhood Recordkeeping in Out of Home Care as an illustrative example. We begin with overviews of the recordkeeping failures of the past and present, and the development of the Charter to address them. We imagine transformed recordkeeping and archiving systems engaging children, young people and Care leavers as creators and decision-makers about their records. We identify challenges and barriers to implementation and discuss the strategies designed to engage major stakeholders in implementing the Charter. The paper concludes by challenging recordkeeping regulators, recordkeeping and archival institutions, current records creators and holders, and the recordkeeping and archival profession to play their essential role in enabling the realisation of this goal and identify the broader relevance of reconceptualising person-centric recordkeeping.

Keywords: *Child-centred recordkeeping*; *Charter of Lifelong Rights in Recordkeeping*; *Recordkeeping systems*; *Strategic intervention*

Prelude: Positioning ourselves in the research

Frank Golding

My interest in the history of institutionalised child welfare arose when I was two years old and charged with the offence of being 'without sufficient means' and I was placed with various foster families and institutions. With the aid of scholarships, I became a teacher and principal in state schools, then worked in teacher education and as a principal policy officer in the Victorian Education Department in the area of social justice and student welfare, and as head of the state's child migrant education programme. Later I managed equal opportunity units at Deakin and Victoria Universities. I am a Life Member of the peak body Care

*Correspondence: Barbara Reed, Email: barbara.reed@recordkeeping.com.au

Leavers Australasia Network (CLAN) and have participated in national projects related to Care leavers and in formal inquiries into out-of-home Care run by the Senate of Australia, the Victorian Parliament, and the Royal Commission into Institutional Responses to Child Sexual Abuse. As a researcher and author, I have presented at national and international conferences. I have a PhD from Federation University Australia. In 2018, I was awarded the Order of Australia Medal (OAM) for service to child welfare and social justice.

Sue McKemmish

My worldview and values were formed during my childhood and are deeply rooted in my Scots, Irish and working-class heritage. Thanks to the introduction of Commonwealth scholarships, I became part of the first generation of first in family university students. I was later recruited by the National Archives of Australia (NAA) and also worked at the Public Record Office Victoria. At NAA, I was involved with a major transfer of records from the Victorian Department of Aboriginal Affairs when responsibility passed to the Commonwealth. Those records are a devastating indictment of the ongoing colonial project in Australia and drove home to me the role that recordkeeping played and is still playing as an instrument of colonialism. Joining Monash in 1990, my research focussed on Records Continuum theory and conceptual modelling, and recordkeeping metadata. More recently, I have focussed on community-centred, participatory recordkeeping and archiving research relating to rights in records, in partnership with those with lived experience of Out of Home Care, and First Nations communities in Australia. Developing inclusive, reflexive research design and practice in partnership with communities is critical to this research. All of the threads have woven together to form the social justice and human rights values and worldview that have motivated and informed my research and education journey.

Barbara Reed

My career has oscillated between the academy, teaching and researching recordkeeping, and the practical implementation of recordkeeping conceptual approaches as a consultant in the field. Archival qualifications preceded immersion in the Australian series system at the National Archives of Australia, followed by practical experience in a range of positions supporting an integrated records and archives approach which became known as recordkeeping. Joining Monash in 1994, I worked with Sue McKemmish, Frank Upward and a range of creative colleagues during the evolution of the records continuum theory. Close involvement in the development of standards for records practice and subsequent instantiation of theory in practice has led to an emphasis on governance controls to support inclusive and expansive recordkeeping informatics. Recent activity has included involvement in person-centric empowerment through recordkeeping in support of human rights and social justice in a range of environments.

Introduction

Years of determined advocacy, the testimony and findings of a string of inquiries, the writings and art of Care leavers, and major research projects have combined to highlight critical recordkeeping failures in the Out-of-Home Care (OOHC) sector. In response, recordkeepers and archivists have worked to overcome structural issues. Concentrating on the records of the past, improvements have been made in processes to ensure the retention of records and to improve access for individuals and their descendants. A degree of participation by those documented in the records has normalised the inclusion of alternative versions or the supplementation of official records. Such responses are seen as a form of institutional redress for the deficiencies of the past. However, the convenient relegation of these problems to history belies the continuation of many of these practices today.

The Australian Research Council-funded project, Charter of Lifelong Rights in Childhood Recordkeeping in Out of Home Care,[1] was a response to the recordkeeping and archival needs of children and young people in Care, and Care leavers. It focussed particularly on non-Indigenous people. Further research is underway to redevelop the Charter to address the specific needs of First Nations children and young people in Care, and to explore the rights-based needs of other stakeholders in the sector – families, foster parents and kinship carers. Customised implementation guidelines have been developed for current record holders and archival institutions, recordkeeping and archival regulators, service providers, social workers and practice case managers in the Care sector, and Care sector regulators. The guidelines include strategies for service providers, case managers and social workers to support children in understanding recordkeeping and participating in the creation and management of their own records. Recordkeeping literacy is conceptualised as a key component of agency and rights for children throughout their lives. Using human rights as foundational framing principles, recordkeeping becomes an instrument to actualise these rights in multiple situations, over considerable time spans. The implementation strategies developed for the Charter also address the role of sectoral leadership and mandates for change, creating strategic levers as part of the systemic requirements on service providers and supporting the interdisciplinary pursuit of significant change in organisational recordkeeping culture and practice.

In this paper, which follows on from a previous paper in *Archives & Manuscripts* titled 'Towards Transformative Practice in Out of Home Care: Chartering Rights in Recordkeeping' (2021), we discuss the challenges encountered when actualising research in practice. We use the implementation of the Charter of Lifelong Rights in Childhood Recordkeeping in Out of Home Care (the Charter), funded by the Australian Research Council and the Jean and Phyllis Whyte Fund, as an illustrative example. We begin with overviews of the recordkeeping failures of the past and present, and the development of the Charter to address them. We imagine transformed recordkeeping and archiving systems engaging children, young people and Care leavers as creators and decision-makers about their records. We then focus on the strategies we designed to engage major stakeholders in implementing the Charter, identifying the barriers we have encountered along the way. We conclude the paper by challenging recordkeeping regulators, recordkeeping and archival institutions, current records creators and holders, and the recordkeeping and archival profession to work with other key stakeholders to play their essential role in enabling the realisation of this goal. As the issues of power imbalance, information inequity, institutional focus and bias are playing out in many systems to the detriment of individuals, the findings of the Charter research project are relevant more broadly. Human rights-based recordkeeping and archiving has the potential to open up significant opportunities for recordkeeping by supporting more humane systems co-design and operation, and extending the application of such approaches to all people-centric recordkeeping systems.

Recordkeeping failures of the past and present
The history of Out of Home Care and associated recordkeeping failures in Australia have been well documented in recent years. From colonial times, actions taken to remove children from family were the result of deliberate social policy driven by racism and classism. While this is clear in the preponderance of working class children removed from family and the forced adoption inflicted on single mothers and children, the most egregious application was the policy to 'breed out indigeneity' and destroy culture for First Nations children who were stolen from their families. For First Nations people, the resulting inter-generational trauma continues to reverberate through the lives of today's children who are conservatively estimated to be 10.4 times more likely to be in OOHC than non-Indigenous children.[2] Groundbreaking

research and development relating to legislative frameworks, policies, programmes, processes and practice for Aboriginal and Torres Strait Islander children and young people in Care and Kinship Care has been undertaken by SNAICC – the National Voice Representing the Rights of Aboriginal and Torres Strait Islander Children.[3]

Frank Golding has been drawing on historical research and lived experience for many years to help expose the consequences of the recordkeeping failures of the past. He recounts how orphanages and children's homes, the mainstay of OOHC in colonial Australia, persisted until the 1980s. They controlled a child's whole being, suppressing their individuality by subjecting them to disciplined routines around food, clothes, sleep, work and play – and, for some but not all, schooling. These institutions limited or forbade contact with family, discounted children's needs or feelings, and subjected them to close surveillance. Recordkeeping was poor or non-existent.

When Care leavers gain access to their files many are shocked by their meagreness, significant gaps and omissions. One person was devastated to find '18 years of my life on two sheets of paper'.[4] Systems-wide deficiencies resulted in failure to track the movements of children and no form of integrated file followed the child through various placements.[5] Care leavers are appalled to find errors ranging from incorrect entry dates and birthdays to serious misrepresentations of facts such as the report of a death which named the wrong sibling. They expect but fail to find reports of their abuse and punishment of offenders, explanations of why they were transferred between institutions, information about siblings and parents, medical incidents and milestones in education. Instead, they are confronted by insulting and disparaging commentary about themselves or their parents, blatant racism, sexism and class bias.[6]

Care leavers also struggle to understand the process of being made a ward of the state. They were not criminals, yet they find in their files that they were charged, convicted, committed – and finally when they aged out, discharged. They are incredulous to find they were removed from their parents for status offences such as being in the company of 'undesirables', 'being in moral danger', deemed to be 'lapsing into a life of vice or crime' or being 'uncontrollable'.[7] The shocking, relentless and pervasive negativity is retraumatising. Care leavers ask: didn't I ever do anything right? Did I never achieve anything when I was a child? The system and its dominant culture regarded them as 'rubbish' children,[8] as reflected in the Director-General of the NSW Child Welfare Department's view in 1960: 'Wards [in NSW] are a selected segment of the juvenile population with a heavy bias towards emotional instability, mental retardation, and inadequacies of character, the consequences of defective home environment in early childhood'.[9]

From the latter half of the twentieth-century, reforms in the Care sector aimed to provide more child-centred Care through foster and kinship Care, and group homes run by not-for-profit and, problematically, profit-making organisations. In 2009, the United Nations issued Guidelines for the Alternative Care of Children.[10] They stated that the assessment, planning and review underpinning decision making on Care 'should involve full consultation at all stages with the child, according to their evolving capacities, and if possible with their parents or legal guardians', with all parties concerned to be provided with the necessary information on which to base their opinion.

Following a plethora of inquiries which exposed the widespread sexual, physical and mental abuse of children in Care, significant reform has occurred in recent times, but it would be a mistake to conclude that the mistakes of the past no longer occur. Most recently, the report of the Commission of Inquiry into the Tasmanian Government's Responses to Child Sexual Abuse in Institutional Settings 2021–2023 reaffirmed the findings of 22 previous reviews on the impacts on children in Care and risks of child abuse associated with poor support for children's involvement in decision making and poor recordkeeping, leading to a recommendation to develop: 'an empowerment and participation strategy for children and young people in out of home care to strengthen children's say in their own care and in the way the out of home care system works'.[11]

Care activists continue to advocate for the child care system, recordkeeping regulators, archival institutions, the recordkeeping profession, current record creators and holders to address the recordkeeping recommendations of past inquiries as a matter of urgency, to act to ensure that recordkeeping supports the agency, wellbeing and dignity of children in Care today, and to break the vicious cycle that condemns Care leavers of the future to experience recordkeeping-associated trauma with at times life-threatening consequences. Agency and participation are critical to a child's growth and wellbeing. Silenced and powerless children are much more likely to suffer abuse.

The experience of children in Australian OOHC, both historically and in current conditions, is specific to Australia.[12] Disturbing echoes can be found worldwide. A range of research-related projects have addressed the challenge of better recordkeeping to empower children in OOHC.[13] Some have prototyped systems enabling children's agency in records,[14] while others have developed functional requirements for system design.[15] Professional responses have been developed, but these largely respond to records of the past.[16]

In our research, we combine ethics of care approaches appropriate to participatory research with communities, with rights-based approaches to transforming recordkeeping practice in the child care sector. We address systemic issues, power imbalances and inequities that continue to oppress the communities we research with. In designing our research, we are guided by the lived experience of significant numbers of children and young people whose Caregivers simply did not care in circumstances where their rights are not recognised or they are subject to abuse. Rights-based approaches aim to bring about systemic change by transforming archival and recordkeeping practices to support the empowerment of those whose voices have been silenced in recordkeeping and archiving, and the actualisation of their human rights. Shifting power balances inevitably involves law and policy reform, regulatory standard setting powers at federal and state levels, people-centred system design and innovative implementation strategies, as well as organisational cultural change. We aim to develop strategic solutions to redress recordkeeping failures and build people-centred recordkeeping and archival systems.[17]

Transforming recordkeeping in the future

To achieve systematic change at all nodes of the extensive child care networked systems, there is a need for an overriding recordkeeping framework in which all participants are focussed on the outcome for the child. The Charter provides one such framework to galvanise and provide a touchstone mandate for change.

What would child-centred recordkeeping look like if it engaged children and young people in records creation and long-term management, and enabled participation in decision making about their Care?

Imagine … children and young people in Care today participating in decision making about all matters that affect their lives, with participation in recordkeeping as a critical enabler. Social workers, foster carers, counsellors and institutional caregivers would include them in decision making and explain that records of that decision making will be made. Information about and participation in recordkeeping are introduced and developed over time. Their views and opinions will be heard and recorded, and the records shown to them as they are created (social worker and counsellor case notes, incident reports, placement reports). They are also told about other records containing information about their time in Care made in different parts of the system, and are informed that these are also their records.

Records are secured in trusted recordkeeping infrastructures which respect both legal and their community concepts of privacy. They are able to ask to look at records at any time and told that these will be accessible or copied for them (except in specific cases where the law currently says not – for example the initial child protection report), including records about their family. They are told about and can get access to records that they are not involved in creating (e.g. records of relevant government departments, contracted third-party providers records, school records, medical and mental health records). They are consulted about requests for access to their records (e.g. for research purposes), and their decisions are recorded and implemented. They are supported in creating their own records as part of their life story. If they decide they want to make their own archive, advice is available on finding third-party applications if systems are not provided in the Care system for this purpose. They can request copies of all records for inclusion in their archive. As part of the process of transitioning out of Care, a safe archiving service is available to them, or they are supported to continue with their third-party application, or to consult with the Australian Orphanage Museum about depositing their records there. They continue to be consulted about requests for access and management decisions related to their records and their decisions are recorded and implemented.

The Charter of Lifelong Rights in Recordkeeping in OOHC

The Charter, primarily developed by Professor Sue McKemmish with Dr Antonina Lewis and Dr Frank Golding, is designed to realise this imagining and Frank Golding's axiomatic principle:

> Every child placed in the custody and control of a welfare agency should absolutely expect that the agency will keep full and accurate records about their experience in Care and in a contemporary situation the child should participate in the process of making and keeping those records.

It is grounded in the lived experience of Care leavers sourced from inquiry testimony and advocacy from Care leavers and members of the Stolen Generations; the voices of children in Care represented in reports of CREATE (an organisation that supports and advocates for children in Care), State Child Commissioners and Guardians, Indigenous service and advocacy organisations, and research findings; and works authored or performed by Care leavers and Stolen Generations, including histories, memoirs, truth telling and artwork. The ultimate goal of the Charter is to embed a construct of the child as having agency and rights to participate in decision making about their lives and related recordkeeping, resulting in transformed archives that include the voices of those who in the past have been powerless captives of the archives (Figure 1).

The Charter and a suite of implementation guidelines are among the major outcomes of the Australian Research Council-funded research project on the lifelong recordkeeping and archival needs of children and young people experiencing Care and their adult selves. The framing rights for the Charter derive from human and cultural rights relating to having a voice in all matters that affect them, remembering and forgetting, identity, truth telling and accountability. Its core principles are child safety and wellbeing, cultural safety, and self-determination linked to archival agency and autonomy. Specific recordkeeping rights include the right for children and young people to participate in recordkeeping that supports decision making in all matters that impact them, including records creation; decision making about access, use, and records retention or destruction; and setting the record straight. This is essential if records are

The challenge of actualising research in practice

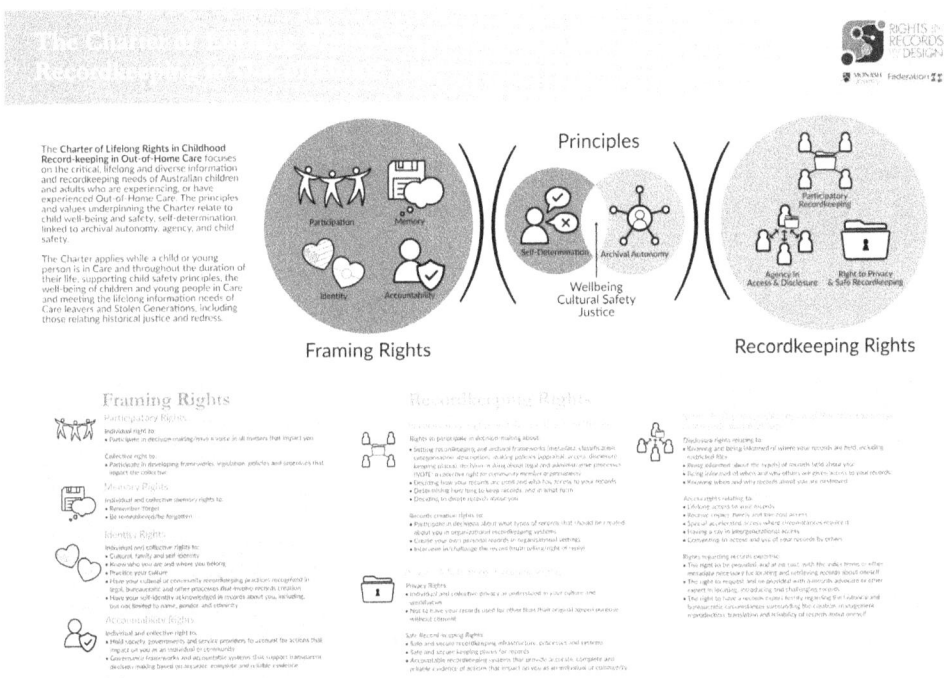

Figure 1. The Charter of Lifelong Rights in Childhood Recordkeeping in Out-of-Home Care.

to be full, accurate and detailed as specified in the Royal Commission's recordkeeping principles.[18] Access rights are vital to well-informed decision making, and are enabled by disclosure rights and rights to access records expertise. Privacy and safe recordkeeping rights ensure that records are only shared with third parties in line with privacy principles, while the provision of safe and sustainable personal recordkeeping and archiving enables children, young people and Care leavers to sustain their own recordkeeping and archiving practices. Child-centred recordkeeping in which children and young people have a voice is critical to improving the quality of recordkeeping and addressing the many failures of recordkeeping in the Care sector. Without the transformation of recordkeeping practice, the trauma and problems currently encountered by Care leavers when trying to access records will be perpetuated.

For children and young people, there is a critical link between participation in recordkeeping, and empowerment, voice and agency. Learning how to participate and take more control of their lives is a significant part of ageing and growing into adults. Participation in this context is:

> … an on-going process of children's expression and active involvement in decision-making at different levels in matters that concern them. It requires information-sharing and dialogue between children and adults based on mutual respect, and that full consideration of their views is given, taking into account the child's age and maturity.[19]

Participation in decision making brings to the process the perspectives of children and young people who have valuable insights to contribute based on their experiences of Care. Their engagement in both decision making and recordkeeping strengthens accountability, and results in better quality records, while developing their capacities as active participants. It is critical to protecting children:

Children who are silenced and passive can be abused by adults with relative impunity. Providing them with information, encouraging them to articulate their concerns and introducing safe and accessible mechanisms for challenging violence and abuse are key strategies for providing effective protection.[20]

Increased participation can also start to address the long-term impacts of the Care system and its recordkeeping which have contributed to the vulnerabilities, disadvantages and poorer life outcomes for those who spend time in Care (including high rates of suicide, poor mental health; a shockingly high level of non-completion of high school, and low levels of participation in higher education).[21]

Implementing the Charter: The challenges and barriers

We are currently engaged with child care activists in an advocacy campaign to convince Australian federal and state archives to use their regulatory standard setting powers to mandate the implementation of the Charter in their jurisdictions. This would be the most effective lever to bring about a transformation of recordkeeping in the sector. Endorsement and promulgation of the Charter of Lifelong Rights in Childhood Recordkeeping in OOHC by key stakeholders would support the reimagined scenario presented above. Implementing the related best practice guidelines would enable rights-based, child-centred recordkeeping. To this end, the research team made presentations to and consulted with many key stakeholders, and made submissions to related commissions, inquiries and reviews.[22]

There is an irony in the work undertaken in developing implementation strategies for the Charter. It is oriented to the individual rights of a child encountering OOHC during their childhood, complemented by collective rights enabling strategic engagement with informed communities of advocacy. The Charter then, has as a primary audience, the child within the OOHC system. Yet our implementation guidelines are, by necessity, aimed not at the child, but at the organisations that are delivering or responsible for the provision of the services. To address this issue, we have built into the relevant guidelines the ways in which case workers and social workers can support children and young people's participation in recordkeeping and the creation of their own archives, including sharing information about OOHC recordkeeping systems, and the existence of third party archival systems and how to access and use them.

The service providers and their regime(s) of regulation provide the frameworks and systems that actually frame the Care for children and are responsible for recordkeeping about and for the child. They determine the rules for recordkeeping which impact the organisational recordkeeping culture in service provider organisations; they provide the monitoring and regulation; and they audit the recordkeeping and report on the implementation of the rules. Thus, the implementation strategy is aimed at both regulators and service provider organisations.

The child protection environment in all states and territories is in flux as models for service delivery are changing in response to clear acknowledgement of defects in past and present models. This is potentially a major barrier to the implementation of the Charter, but also a possible lever given the broader push for change towards a more child-centred OOHC system. Another barrier is the fact that State-provided services are now largely managed by contracted service providers with contract monitoring and oversight provided by state and territory provisioning agencies, a model endorsed as the most appropriate for service provision in the most recent 2023 Tasmanian Inquiry.[23] Contracts for services require reporting and performance standards. Service providers can be provisioned in and out. Carers are licensed to service providers. Locating service provision in communities, or with specialist service providers can result in uncertainty impacting organisational continuity, producing vastly complex distributed recordkeeping responsibilities. The ecosystem of nested contractual obligations and recordkeeping responsibilities distributed across an ever-changing array of providers is another implementation barrier. Introducing a model that allows for-profit making within the system also complicates and potentially increases instability within the service provider operatives. For children seeking to assert recordkeeping rights over time, this means navigating a hugely problematic and badly connected set of potential records creating bodies. Difficult both to understand and trace over time, the recordkeeping implications of such complex structures are daunting even to those within the system, let alone a child attempting to assert recordkeeping rights.

As in many contemporary operating environments, there is an implicit assumption that technology will provide the key. These techno solutionist[24] approaches envisage quick and 'flawless' ways to solve complex real-world problems that in fact are better addressed by social approaches. Too many promises are made by technologists and vendors, with a focus on organisation-centric and superficial change, often at the whim of the market. Recordkeeping requirements are rarely front of mind in such situations, with the result that vendors are effectively colonising Australian practice with the end-of-life assumptions about managing records (where this is considered at all). Technology approaches are therefore not a productive locus for attaining strategic recordkeeping outcomes. While such systems must have their place, these should be considered the end point of a reimagined means to implement change, and should be deployed to serve these requirements, rather than being the immediate 'fix'. To enable children in Care to realise their lifelong requirements for records, the need for sustainable records across multiple technologies, employed by multiple service providers and multiple layers of monitoring and reporting, must be well understood and designed into these systems.

Recordkeeping voices are largely silent here. As a sector, recordkeeping professionals have yet to stand up and seriously advocate for change to organisational mindsets and requirements to assist in creating the environments needed to assert human rights in records. This is an ongoing challenge but one that everyone involved with recordkeeping must step up to. While business and industry may broadly understand specific processes and be able to identify user requirements for records in specific processes, recordkeeping professionals can specifically add advocacy for future requirements to extend recordkeeping beyond the immediate here and now.

To date, interventions from recordkeeping regulators have also been inadequate or ineffective. For example, the Royal Commission into Institutional Responses to Child Sexual Abuse dedicated a whole volume of the final report to recordkeeping. It included proactive statements of recordkeeping principles and commended these to all organisations involved in the child protection environment. At a strategic level, recordkeeping was almost immediately brought in under the umbrella of Child Safe standards by the Australian Human Rights Commission, with recordkeeping explicitly addressed as a subsidiary component to Principle 7 of those standards.[25] As each state and territory created their own versions of the Child Safe Standards in their jurisdiction-specific legislation or regulation, even this oblique attention to records was lost. Somehow all records needs are now subsumed into complaints processes. This is not the empowered vision that the Royal Commission recommended for recordkeeping, and, frustratingly, it appears that the strategic importance of records is no longer a front-of-mind consideration within jurisdiction-based child-safe standards and charters of children's rights.

Implementation strategies: Top down, bottom up and external

In recognition of the reality of organisations – including inherent complexities, shifting dynamics and complex nested components – developing implementation strategies for the Charter focussed on actions that could be achieved here and now. Realistic expectations about the speed of change are acknowledged,[26] with the publication of the Charter and the release of toolkits only the beginning of a long process.

Multiple strategies have been adopted to assist the implementation of change required to make the Charter a reality for children in the OOHC system. These strategies primarily focus on creating mandates for action, and targeting the policies and procedural layers within organisations. Locating implementation here can effectively address expectations, change behaviours and enable flexibility to encompass incremental change. It also enables focus on what can be done now, in the hands of practitioners. Practice then changes organisational culture, strategic focus and hopefully, over time, technology requirements.

The implementation strategies for the Charter can be crudely characterised as comprising top down, bottom up and external levers. An endorsement strategy creates the mandate – the top down approach. A toolkit for implementation has been published,[27] addressing the bottom up and pragmatic action agenda. Oversight, audit and monitoring of recordkeeping is recommended as an outside-in strategy from recordkeeping and children and young people's regulators can create the levers for change. Care leavers and advocates continue to revisit and reinterpret their experiences, as outlined above, and thus create what might be characterised as part of the inside-out/outside-in strategies.

Endorsement strategy – Top down

The primary top down strategy pursued is endorsement of the Charter. The aim is to create a mandate for specific jurisdictions to implement the Charter. This requires involvement from key players in the OOHC sector, identified as: the regulators and monitors of the child protection systems; the government departments responsible for OOHC administration; advocacy organisations engaged in improving children's recordkeeping; selected care provision agencies and the recordkeeping regulators. We started by reaching out to those who have previously engaged with academic research through attendance at the 2017 National Summit,[28] including requests for targeted recommendations that could be used for snowballing. Additional direct contact was made with each of the Children and Young People's Guardians and Commissioners and recordkeeping regulators. The recordkeeping regulators (State and Territory archives and records authorities) are those responsible for the recordkeeping frameworks in place for each jurisdiction and are our own known community. Professional peak bodies for records and key advocacy bodies for children were also included in the endorsement strategy.

The invitations provided a clear outline of the Charter, its intentions, and aspirations, and also included an offer for a briefing session. Briefings conducted by McKemmish and Reed, with specific expertise provided, where possible, by Golding, were presented to eight Children's Commissioners and Guardians at federal, state and territory levels, including sessions for Aboriginal and Torres Strait Islander Commissioners where independent positions existed. Each session outlined the background and development of the Charter, the importance of recordkeeping for children in Care, a high-level view of the rights identified and details of implementation guidelines. Explicit invitations to endorse the Charter were extended, with endorsement received from four Commissioners and Guardians to date.

A similar strategy was pursued with recordkeeping regulators and peak recordkeeping bodies. CAARA, ASA and RIMPA have endorsed the Charter, as have four State and Territory archives (including NZ), one Information Commissioner and one Privacy Commissioner.

Others stated that their implicit endorsement was included in their engagement with the peak bodies. The two key advocacy bodies for children in OOHC, CLAN and CREATE, have also explicitly endorsed the Charter.

There are some indications levels of endorsement could be directly linked to the circumstances of OOHC in various jurisdictions. All involved with the sector know the complexities and embedded problems with the ways current systems deliver OOHC. Specific inquiries were underway or recently completed in a number of jurisdictions. Media reporting has kept the issues and problems in front of the public's attention. Jurisdictions with direct, recent experience of reviews were more receptive to adopting the Charter as one mechanism to affect change. Experience with inadequate or inaccurate recordkeeping also seemed to affect which jurisdictions were open to engagement, at both Commissioner/Guardian and government department levels. We actively pursued engagement with those who were most interested, with the hope that those less engaged would follow industry leaders.

Similar considerations determined engagement with recordkeeping regulators. In that community there were some perceptible concerns about adopting a Charter which was clearly aspirational: that is, the Charter outlined what was wanted and needed, rather than what was in place. Other hypothesised concerns included the extent to which the Charter's provisions could be monitored or required by the recordkeeping regulators.

At the time of writing this strategy has led to endorsement of the Charter by 16 key organisations.[29] However, endorsement is in itself relatively easy. Does it make a difference? Has it had a lasting impact on the systems within jurisdictions that have endorsed it? Can children in Care use the Charter to assert their rights? How can implementation be achieved and measured? Knowing the difficulties involved in all of these areas led to the development of further implementation guidance.

Best practice guidance and practice guides – Bottom up

Our experience to date suggests that organisations seeking to implement the Charter require more directed assistance than simply being asked to endorse the framework. The Implementation Toolkit (Figure 2) attempts to address this through a Best Practice Guideline aimed largely at the strategic management of service providers. This links specific recordkeeping rights to the indicators of best practice and to the pragmatic practice guides which support it.

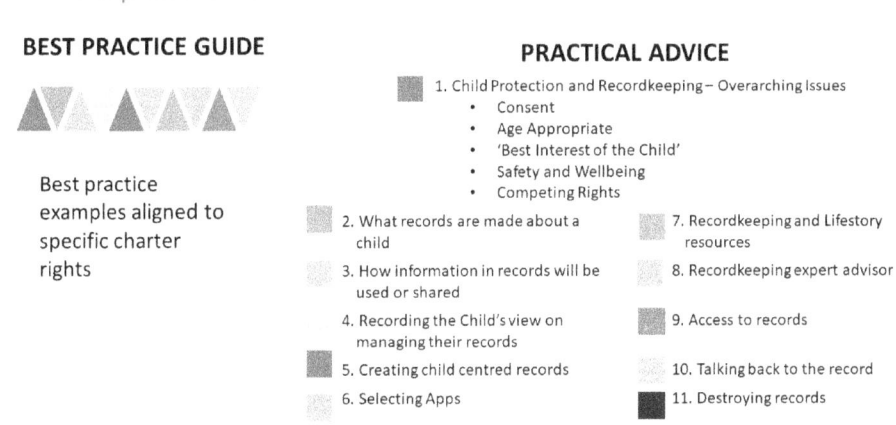

Figure 2. Implementation toolkit overview.

The Guidelines use the testimony of survivors of OOHC to emphasise the impact that will be provided by actualising those rights.

Reed developed a set of 11 Practice Guides aimed at service provider practitioners and recordkeeping specialists. These provide a summary discussion of why specific recordkeeping actions will improve practice, what best practice looks like and how they can be implemented, along with links to further resources to enable further exploration.

The Practice Guides push the boundaries of both social workers' practice and existing recordkeeping paradigms. They also acknowledge the significant changes seen in the social work profession, which has worked to create records that are child centred, paying attention to the importance of language, stressing the positive and remaining child-focussed. These aspects of social work are brought into focus in Practice Guide 5: Creating Child Centred Records. Extending changes in writing records are practices for sharing the record with the child (and family, if relevant) at the time of record creation. The intention here is to enable transparency, demystify 'the system', and ensure the appropriate capture of the right details and relevant information, potentially removing many downstream problems. If a child knows and participates in decision making and what has been written about them, can see the resulting records about them, knows their views have been incorporated, and can obtain copies, the access problems that have so plagued older Care leavers virtually disappear. Similarly, some of the daunting monolithic barriers of 'the welfare' bureaucracy are demystified and dismantled if there is transparency about what records are created, and where this happens in the complex ecosystem of child protection (Practice Guide 2: What records are kept about me?); and knowledge about information sharing practices embedded in the system, along with processes for obtaining explicit consent where sharing is not mandatory (Practice Guide 3: How information in records will be used or shared with others).

An individual recordkeeping plan supporting children and young people is outlined in Practice Guide 4. Plans are seemingly the backbone of child protection services, and while notably observed in the breach, this new addition to the planning regime provides a mechanism for recording the wishes of the children concerning their decisions about their records – what they want to be kept, whether and how they wish to receive copies of records, access permissions, and consent and destruction of records. These are rights outlined in the Charter, and the plan is a way of ensuring such rights are renewed, kept up to date and available for the organisation to monitor implementation.

Recordkeeping rights are quite complex. Understanding both the ecosystem of interrelated organisations that provide, commission and monitor OOHC, how to record individual requirements in a plan, and the long-term implications for some decisions requires support for the child. Access to records requires knowledge of where the records are – the right of disclosure. To support individual children navigating these issues, a new role – the recordkeeping expert advisor – has been developed. Their job is to advocate for the child, ensuring that their wishes are implemented and supporting decision making in relation to records (e.g., a requirement that an individual's records be destroyed once they leave Care). Recordkeeping professionals may not always be the best people to fill this role. As with supported access to records, a deeply knowledgeable social worker may be more appropriate, trained to be both an empathetic communicator with the child and an advocate for that child in asserting recordkeeping rights (Practice Guide 8: Recordkeeping Expert Advisor).

Activating recordkeeping rights for children in Care challenges some of the recordkeeping norms. These include how records are created, and changing the focus to centre the child, not the organisation. Granular definitions of rights affecting the management of records defy what current recordkeeping systems are designed to do, and what practitioners take as normal practice. These include rights relating to access, privacy, ownership and approval for information sharing.

Similarly, authorising the destruction of records by the child (supported by a recordkeeping expert advisor, as outlined in Practice Guide 11) is deeply challenging to many recordkeepers. The Practice Guides aim to create sufficient context to enable recordkeeping practitioners to act on behalf of the child, in conjunction with changing social work practice.

Strategies for regulators – Outside in
The implementation strategies above focus on the Charter as a mandate (top down), and the identification of best practices through pragmatic guides (bottom up). As discussed, changes can be frustratingly slow to implement, particularly where recordkeeping is largely invisible to achieving strategic outcomes for children. Regulators have a specific role to play in creating momentum to facilitate organisational change. This creates an outside-in implementation strategy.

Specifically, both the children and young people's regulators and the recordkeeping regulators can provide mechanisms to promote action in supporting recordkeeping rights. Reed developed two Implementation Strategies (Figures 3 and 4), one for each set of regulators, to suggest 9 pragmatic actions that each could implement now to support changes in recordkeeping practice within organisations supporting children in OOHC.
As yet, there is little indication that any such strategies have been implemented, despite the endorsement of the Charter.

Testing organisational reactions in training
Working with one of the implementation partners in this research, Child and Family Services (CAFS) at Ballarat, the team of Dr David McGinniss and Ember Parkin of Ashtree Projects developed training sessions using the research outcomes. Anecdotal reactions, particularly to the training on better ways to create records (Practice Guide 5: Creating child centred records, and Practice Guide 7: Recordkeeping and Lifestory Resources), immediately identified that the practices outlined were not only of relevance to children in OOHC but to all recordkeeping for all the services that CAFS supports.

This was a very heartening response. Once the importance of recordkeeping is contextualised within a service such as CAFS, it can become a central plank for delivering lifelong support to anyone assisted by their services. CAFS conceptualises all these people as current and ongoing clients. The relevance of current practice and responsibility for the long term is seen as a continuing commitment – something for which recordkeeping is a fundamental support. The ease with which the participants realised the broader impacts of recordkeeping rights on individuals and their life chances inspires hope that widespread adoption of human rights-based recordkeeping is possible.

Rising to the challenge
Archival institutions could use their current recordkeeping regulatory, standard setting and advisory roles to support children and young people in Care today and into the future. They could:

- Endorse the Charter
- Work with Children and Young People's Commissioners to develop specific guidelines for creating full, accurate, reliable and authentic records that include the voices of children and young people in the OOHC sector
- Develop a standard for relevant government agencies across all jurisdictions relating to implementing the Charter
- Provide a child-centred, participatory recordkeeping role model for government agencies
- Require contracts for outsourcing to private sector providers to include the provision for implementing the Charter and eventually depositing related organisational records with State or Territory archival institutions

Charter of Lifelong Rights in Childhood Recordkeeping in Out-of-Home Care

Implementation Strategies for Recordkeeping Regulators

Records kept for and about children in Out of Home Care have an impact for a lifetime. Empowering children to participate in decision making and recordkeeping, to know about and have free access to records throughout their time in Care and at any time in their life can significantly affect life chances. Recognising this, Recordkeeping Regulators can constructively engage with all layers of the child protection system to enable child-centric recordkeeping.

Endorse/Adopt	Develop	Pilot
1 **Endorse and promulgate the Charter** of Lifelong Rights in Childhood Recordkeeping in Out-of-Home Care. The Charter provides a mandate for reconceptualised child-centred recordkeeping.	**4** **Develop**, in conjunction with peer organisations, **National Standard on Recordkeeping for children in Out-of-Home Care** aligned to Child Safe Standards. Cross jurisdictional, national recordkeeping standards enable consistency and a focus on child-centred recordkeeping.	**7** Work with partner organisation to **pilot implementation of national standard.** Provide proactive support to early adopting service providers.
2 **Endorse and promulgate Best Practices Guidance** for Service Providers - within and between jurisdictions. Adopting uniform Best Practice Guidance for Service Providers focusses recordkeeping on requirements of children.	**5** **Develop jurisdictional arrangements for ensuring long term retention** of service provider records. Orphaned records, left with private organisations which may or may not continue to provide Out-of-Home Care services have been clearly identified as a problem for children leaving Care. Incorporating proactive measures to provide long term maintenance and access to these records is required across all jurisdictions.	**8** **Work with Children and Young People sector Regulators to develop audit methodology** for recordkeeping for children and young people. CYP Regulators monitor and investigate service provider practices on behalf of children – incorporating recordkeeping into these processes assists implementation of best practice.
3 **Support implementation of Best Practice Toolkit.** The Toolkit addresses consistency of practice and identifies achievable improvements in practice.	**6** **Develop model recordkeeping contract clauses** for service providers of OOHC. Service providers need contractually binding requirements for recordkeeping, during and after contract terms.	**9** Practical guidance on maintaining records through technology system change. Service Providers need practical assistance to ensure reliable records across systems changes

Figure 3. Implementation strategies for recordkeeping regulators.

If archives are open to learning the lessons of the past and present, and dare to take transformative action to realise a reimagined future, the experiences of children and young people in Care and Care leavers could be very different from those described in the first part of this paper. It is not as though there is a shortage of warrants for such action in the United Nations Guidelines for Alternative Care, the

Charter of Lifelong Rights in Childhood Recordkeeping in Out-of-Home Care

Implementation Strategies for Children and Young People Commissioners or Regulators

> ...every child placed in the custody and control of a welfare agency should absolutely expect that the agency will keep full and accurate records about their experience in Care (and in a contemporary situation the child should participate in the process of making and keeping those records) Frank Golding

Endorse/Adopt	Incorporate	Review
1 **Endorse and promulgate Charter** of Lifelong Rights in Childhood Recordkeeping in Out of Home Care. The Charter provides a mandate for reconceptualised child-centred recordkeeping.	**4** Include **recordkeeping** in all reviews and monitoring of services. Child-centred recordkeeping is a key component of all services. Incorporating recordkeeping in all reviews and monitoring activity ensures on-going attention to recordkeeping is adopted in practice.	**7** Conduct **recordkeeping audits** on departments and Contracted Service Providers. Working with Recordkeeping Regulators to develop practical audit methodologies enables effective reviews of practice.
2 **Incorporate recordkeeping into existing Charters** of Rights for Children and Young People. Update existing Charters to include, at minimum, a reference to children's rights in records.	**5** Ensure **contracts for service provision and carers include lifelong recordkeeping** rights for children. Advocate for use of recordkeeping model contract clauses and monitor their implementation in practice.	**8** Audit arrangements to ensure that records will be **accessible for the child's lifetime.** Attention to life-long accessibility of records reinforces requirements beyond current systems.
3 **Recommend adoption** of Charter (and Recordkeeping Best Practices Guidance) for all service providers. Promulgate recordkeeping improvement using best practice guidance to all providers as part of the protective framework for children.	**6** Ensure **recordkeeping is explicitly addressed** in practice manuals, guidance to contracted service providers, carers. Recordkeeping should be clearly specified and embedded in practices at all levels of the child protection system.	**9** Call out **recordkeeping deficits** where they impede either reviews or rights of children and young people. Explicitly referencing recordkeeping deficiencies or good practice in reviews keeps recordkeeping visible as a protective mechanism for children and young people.

Figure 4. Implementation strategies for Children and Young People Commissioners or Regulators.

National Framework for Protecting Australia's Children 2009–2020 endorsed by the Council of Australian Governments,[30] the findings of all the federal and state inquiries and reviews, Care leaver testimonies and publications, the research reports and so on.

If they do dare, Care leavers accessing their files will no longer be shocked by their absence or meagreness. They will not be confronted with dossiers made in secret by the people who controlled their lives, in which their voices were silenced. They will no longer be appalled to find so many gaps, omissions and misrepresentations. Their expectations of finding why they were transferred between institutions, information about siblings and parents, medical incidents and milestones in education will be met. Records will no longer include insulting and disparaging commentary about them or their parents, or blatant racism, sexism and class bias. The shocking negativity will be replaced by records that include happy times, achievements and talents, as well as more challenging content. And most important of all, children and young people in Care will become recordkeeping agents participating in improving the quality of recordkeeping and calling all those responsible for providing quality Care to account.

Towards the future: Human-centred, rights-based recordkeeping and archiving
Recordkeeping professionals working with child care advocates with lived experience have reimagined recordkeeping as a core component of Care, enabling ongoing participation in how the children in Care are represented in records, and how records are created, managed and accessed, to enable assertions of human rights embodied in recordkeeping rights. As we imagine the ways in which recordkeeping rights can be implemented, it is evident that the same rights and the same issues are being experienced through recordkeeping relating to all people.

Children in Care are in a position of extreme vulnerability, and not all people experience systemic vulnerability to the same extent. But anyone, and potentially everyone, will be enmeshed in systematised recordkeeping, whether hidden behind the increasing social surveillance imposed through technologies such as facial recognition, or through exposure to algorithmic decision making and the obsessive data collection associated with everything from web browsing to using our cars.[31]

The recent report of the Royal Commission into the Robodebt Scheme[32] exposed the vulnerability of people being assessed by the ethically dubious application of machine learning technologies. As is common knowledge, the way this harsh practice was implemented led to multiple suicides. While not tested, it is expected that there will be an intersection between Care leavers and those caught up in the Robodebt scheme. And the harms inflicted by using data badly, particularly against people who have been stigmatised or marginalised in some way, are not restricted to Australia. For example, over 20,000 people in the Netherlands faced similar harms when falsely accused of fraud related to the distribution of Child Care benefits through ethically flawed and racist means.[33] The Danish government's use of machine learning to identify these welfare recipients are eerily similar to the Robodebt scheme.[34]

Where data, information and records are potentially weaponised against citizens – often the most marginalised and vulnerable citizens – the need for individuals to redress the power imbalances inherent in such practices becomes critical. The lessons learnt from working with children in Care in relation to recordkeeping rights and the ability to assert those rights could become a significant challenge to the way recordkeeping professionals conceptualise their practice. Enabling individuals to challenge 'the system' will require quite different thinking about ownership, stewardship and custodianship of records and information. Future recordkeeping systems which enable recordkeeping rights will look quite different to the organisational repositories now in place.

The implications for the broader recordkeeping and archival sector are far-reaching. For example, recordkeeping and archival education and training programmes would need to include a curriculum relating to: actualising participatory rights in recordkeeping and archiving for all those involved in the activities documented in records; people- and community-centred rather than organisation-centric recordkeeping system co-design and implementation; and strategies for effecting cultural change in institutional archives and organisational settings. There might be a similar shift in the work consultants do in organisations, and hopefully increasingly with communities, and in archival and recordkeeping standards now and into the future. There are implications too for the future research required to support significant change, including comparative studies of initiatives in different global contexts, and strategies to mitigate the problematic service provision issues that arise in Care sectors increasingly driven by profitmaking motives.

Centring human rights and recordkeeping rights offers a very different view of the professional responsibilities of recordkeeping professionals, institutional archives and organisational recordkeeping. As a professional community, there is a chance to make a different future for rights-based recordkeeping, but to do so will need strong and courageous leadership, cultural change, reconceptualisation of roles, systems and tools, and the willingness to rise to the challenge.

Acknowledgements
Funding for research on the Charter of Lifelong Rights in Childhood Recordkeeping in Out of Home Care has been provided by the Jean and Phyllis Whyte Fund (Faculty of Information Technology, Monash University) and the Rights in Records by Design Project through an Australian Research Council (ARC) Discovery Grant DP170100198: Chief Investigators Associate Professor Joanne Evans (Monash University), Associate Professor Jacqueline Wilson (Federation University Australia), Professor Sue McKemmish (Monash University), Associate Professor Philip Mendes (Monash University), Professor Keir Reeves (Federation University Australia) and Dr Jane Bone (Monash University), with postdoctoral fellow Dr Gregory Rolan (Monash University) and research fellow Dr Frank Golding OAM (CLAN and Federation University). CLAN and the Community and Family Services (CAFS) regional office in Ballarat have been community partners in the project.

The Charter's development was endorsed by the 2017 *National Summit on Setting the Record Straight for the Rights of the Child*. The National Summit was convened by Monash University in partnership with Care Leavers Australasia Network (CLAN), an advocacy and support group for older Care leavers; the Child Migrants Trust, an advocacy and support service for child migrants/deportees from Britain and its colonial posts; Connecting Home, a service for the Stolen Generation; the CREATE Foundation, the national consumer body representing children and young people with Care experience; Federation University Australia and the University of Melbourne.

Members of the research team who developed the Charter were Dr Frank Golding OAM, Dr Antonina Lewis, Professor Sue McKemmish, Barbara Reed and Dr Greg Rolan. The suite of implementation guidelines for the Charter was developed by Barbara Reed. Dr David McGinniss (formerly Federation University, now Melbourne University) and Ember Parkin developed related training materials and worked closely with community partner Child and Family Services (CAFS) Ballarat in the project.

Notes on contributors
Frank Golding is an Honorary Research Fellow at Federation University Australia, where he completed a PhD entitled Care Leavers Recovering Voice and Agency through Counter-Narrative, and a Life Member of Care Leavers Australasia Network (CLAN), the national Care leaver advocacy body. A social historian, Frank has contributed to formal inquiries dealing with the institutionalisation of children and to projects with the National Museum, the National Library of Australia and the National Summit on Rights in

Records. He has written more than a dozen books, as well as book chapters and refereed journal articles and has presented papers on child welfare in the UK and several European countries.

Sue McKemmish Joining Monash in 1990, Sue McKemmish's research focussed on Records Continuum theory and conceptual modelling, and recordkeeping metadata. Her Records Continuum theory-building and modelling work has continued throughout her career. More recently, she has focussed on community-centred, participatory recordkeeping and archiving research relating to rights in records, complemented by ethics of care, in response to advocacy by those with lived experience of Out-of-Home Care, and First Nations peoples in Australia. Developing inclusive, reflexive research design and practice in partnership with communities has been a critical part of this research.

Barbara Reed is currently working as a part-time Research Fellow on the Rights in Records projects of Monash University. As an independent archives and records consultant she has worked with a range of government, non-government, private and non-profit organisations, in Australia and internationally. Much of her work has been focussed on developing recordkeeping practices and competencies, transforming recordkeeping into digital practice, and working with a range of stakeholders to create strategic interventions through standards and best practice guidelines. She has taught archives and records subjects at a number of Australian Universities.

ORCID

Sue McKemmish
Barbara Reed

Notes

1. Development of the Charter has been funded as part of the ARC Rights in Records by Design Project, available at https://rights-records.it.monash.edu/research-development-agenda/rights-in-records-by-design/recordkeeping-rights-charter/, accessed 18 February 2024. We use the term Care with a capital C ironically as the Care system has failed to care for many generations of children. OOHC references any child who has been removed from family - orphans, children in orphanages, and children's Homes, child migrants sent to Australia after World War II , and those in more recent forms of statutory care (kinship, foster and residential care).
2. SNAICC, Family Matters Report, 2022, available at http://www.snaicc.org.au/wp-content/uploads/2023/09/221123_16_Growing-Up-Strong-Children-1.pdf, accessed 18 February 2024.
   These figures vary by jurisdiction. The most recent figures published by the Victorian Yoorook Justice Commission identified that, in 2023, First Nations children were 5.7 times as likely to be the subject to a report to child protection services; 7.6 times as likely to have finalised investigation by child protection services, 8.5 times as likely to be found to be 'in need of protection' by child protection services and 21.7 times as likely to be in out of home care.
   Yoorrook Justice Commission, Yoorrook for Justice. Report into Victoria's Child Protection and Criminal Justice Systems, 2023
3. SNAICC, Understanding and Applying the Aboriginal and Torres Strait Islander Child Placement Principle: A Resource for Legislation, Policy and Program Development, SNAICC, Eltham Victoria, 2017, available at https://www.snaicc.org.au/wp-content/uploads/2017/07/Understanding_applying_ATSICCP.pdf, accessed 18 February 2024; SNAICC Values Statement on Children's Rights, available at https://www.snaicc.org.au/about/vision-and-purpose/values-statement-aboriginal-torres-strait-islander-children/, accessed 2021.
4. Senate Community Affairs References Committee, Forgotten Australians: A Report on Australians Who Experienced Institutional or Out-of-home Care as Children, Commonwealth of Australia, Canberra, 2004, Submission 3.
5. The Committee of Inquiry into Child Care Services in Victoria (Norgard Report) (1976) commented that 'The Department's present provisions for record-keeping and reviewing progress of its wards requires

thorough overhaul'. In 1991, John Paterson, the Department's Director-General, described the system as 'pitiful', CSV, Annual Report 1991, Melbourne, p. 10.
6. F. Golding and J.Z. Wilson, 'Lost and Found: Counter Narratives of Dis/located Children', in Kristine Moruzi , Nell Musgrove, & Carla Pascoe Leahy(eds.), Children's Voices from the Past: New Historical and Interdisciplinary Perspectives, Palgrave Macmillan, Cham, 2019, pp. 305–329.
7. Senate Standing Committee on Social Welfare, Children in Institutional and Other Forms of Care-A national perspective, Commonwealth of Australia, Canberra, ACT, 1985, p. 11.
8. D. Jaggs, Interviewed by Jill Barnard in the Forgotten Australians and Former Child Migrants Oral History Project, National Library of Australia, Canberra, ACT, 2011, Session 1 of 6, available at http://catalogue.nla.gov.au/Record/5079534?lookfor=Donella%20Jaggs&offset=1&max=9, accessed 18 February 2024.
9. R.H. Hicks, 'Public and Voluntary Child Welfare Services in New South Wales, International Child Welfare Review vol. XIV, 1960 qu', in J. Penglase (ed.), Orphans of the Living: Growing Up in 'care' in Twentieth-Century Australia, Curtin University Books, Fremantle, 2005, p. 233.
10. UN General Assembly, Guidelines for the Alternative Care of Children, Resolution Adopted by the General Assembly: A/RES/64/142, 2010
11. Commission of Inquiry into the Tasmanian Government's Responses to Child Sexual Abuse in Institutional Settings 2021–2023, 2023, Volume 4.2
12. C. Tilbury and J. Thoburn , 'Children in Out-of-Home Care in Australia – International Comparisons', Children Australia, vol. 33, no. 3, pp. 5–12, 2008. See also, for example, The Danish Welfare Museum (Danmarks Forsorgsmuseum), University College Copenhagen (Københavns Professionshøjskole), The Danish National Archives (Rigsarkivet) and TABUKA - The Association of Children placed in care and care-leavers. 'The Right to your own history' You Tube, 2023, available at https://youtu.be/z8b5Zgi2M9g, accessed 18 February 2024.
13. For example, Professor Joanne Evans, Rights in Records by Design project from Monash University, 2015–2019, available at https://rights-records.it.monash.edu/research-development-agenda/rights-in-records-by-design/, accessed 18 February 2024; The MIRRA project. Memory-Identity- Rights in Records – Access 2017–2021, University College London, available at https://blogs.ucl.ac.uk/mirra/about/, accessed 18 February 2024.
14. G. Rolan, H.D. Phan, and J. Evans, 'Recordkeeping and Relationships: Designing for Lifelong Information Rights.' in DIS '20: Proceedings of the 2020 ACM Designing Interactive Systems Conference, Eindhoven Netherlands July, 2020; E. Shepherd, V. Hoyle, E. Lomas, and A. Finn, 'Towards a Human-Centered Participatory Approach to Child Social Care Recordkeeping', Archives and Museum Informatics, vol 20, no. 3-4, 2020.
15. E. Shepherd, A. Sexton, E. Lomas, P. Williams, M. Denton, and T. Marchant, 'A Participatory Recordkeeping Application Software Requirement Specifications (SRS)', MIRRA research project, 2021, available at https://doi.org/10.5281/zenodo.5599430, accessed 18 February 2024.
16. For example, CAARA, Maximising Access to Care Leavers' Records, November 2021, available at https://www.caara.org.au/wp-content/uploads/2022/04/Maximising-Access-To-Care-Leavers-Records-Version-1.1.pdf, accessed 18 February 2024, or ICA, Section on Archives and Human Rights, Access rights of adults to documents relating to their own childhood experience of adoption or being in care, DRAFT, February 2024.
17. We note that ethics of care research methods should not be confused with radical empathy in the context of feminist ethics of care. The latter has been proposed as an alternative to rights-based approaches by Michelle Caswell and Marika Cifor. More recently they have discussed how empathetic archivists could also engage in dismantling oppressive structures and rebuilding liberatory structures. We view rights vs radical empathy as a false binary, opting instead for the transformative power of combining the ethics of care with rights based strategies. In our view, rejecting rights approaches in favour of feminist ethics of care is too dependent on the work of empathetic archivists and their capacity to effect scaleable, systemic change in the structures in which they are embedded. See: M. Caswell and M. Cifor, 'From Human Rights to Feminist Ethics: Radical Empathy in the Archives', Archivaria, vol. 81, Spring 2016, pp. 23–43; M. Caswell and M. Cifor, 'Revisiting an Ethics of Care in Archives: An Introductory Note', in Elvia Arroyo-Ramirez, Jasmine Jones, Shannon O'Neill, and Holly Smith (eds.), Radical Empathy in Archival Practice, Special issue, Journal of Critical Library and Information Studies, vol. 3, no. 2, 2021, available at https://journals.litwinbooks.com/index.php/jclis/article/view/162, accessed 18 February 2024.
18. Royal Commission on Institutional Responses to Child Sexual Abuse, 2017. Adoption of the child safety principles in all organisations was recommended by the Royal Commission into Institutional Responses to Child Sexual Abuse 2017, and they are incorporated in the Australian Human Rights Commission, National Principles for Child Safe Organisations, Australian Human Rights Commission, 2018 and the

Framework for Protecting Australia's Children 2009–2020, available at https://childsafe.humanrights.gov.au/national-principles, accessed 18 February 2024.

19. EU-UNICEF, Child Rights Toolkit: Integrating Child Rights in Development Cooperation, New York, 2014, Module 3, p. 5.
20. Ibid., p. 6.
21. P. Mendes, J. Purtell, and G. Armstrong, 'Examining the Role of Lived Experience Consultants in an Australian Research Study on the Educational Experiences of Children and Young People in Out-of-Home Care', Qualitative Social Work, vol. 22, no. 5, 2022.
22. For information about endorsement of the Charter, see https://www.monash.edu/it/clrc/endorsement; and https://www.monash.edu/it/clrc/publications for a list of submissions, accessed 18 February 2024.
23. Commission of Inquiry into the Tasmanian Government's Responses to Child Sexual Abuse in Institutional Settings 2021–2023 (2023), Volume 4.2, Recommendation 9.2, p. 87.
24. Schull, n.d., 'The Folly of Technological Solutionism: An Interview with Evgeny Morozov, Public Books' in Evgeny Morozov (ed.), To Save Everything, Click Here: The Folly of Technological Solutionism, Farrar, Straus and Giroux, New York, 2013.
25. 'Principle 7: Staff and volunteers are equipped with the knowledge, skills and awareness to keep children and young people safe through ongoing education and training', with specific indicator requiring 'Staff and volunteers receive training on the rights of children and young people in relation to records being created about children and young people and their use' Australian Human Rights Commission, 2018.
26. The time it takes to implement change is demonstrated by the DSS Guidelines for Access, a project in which two of the authors were significantly engaged. Developed in 2014, publicly available since 2015, full implementation is still not achieved in 2023, despite continuous endorsement from Royal Commissions and Commissions of Inquiry. Recordkeeping Innovation on behalf of the Department of Social Services, 2015.
27. The Implementation Toolkit is available at https://www.monash.edu/it/clrc/toolkit
28. National Summit, Setting the Record Straight for the Rights of the Child, May 2017, available at https://rights-records.it.monash.edu/summit/may-2017-national-summit-outcomes/, accessed 18 February 2024.
29. Endorsements are included on the project web pages, available at https://www.monash.edu/it/clrc/endorsement, accessed 18 February 2024.
30. UN General Assembly, Guidelines for the Alternative Care of Children, Resolution adopted by the General Assembly: A/RES/64/142, 2010, Australian Human Rights Commission, 2018.
31. J. Caltrider, M. Rykov, and Z. MacDonald, 'It's Official. Cars are the Worst Product Category We Have Ever Reviewed for Privacy', Mozilla News, 2023, available at https://foundation.mozilla.org/en/privacynotincluded/articles/its-official-cars-are-the-worst-product-category-we-have-ever-reviewed-for-privacy/, accessed 18 February 2024.
32. Royal Commission into the Robodebt Scheme, Report 2023, available at https://robodebt.royalcommission.gov.au/publications/report, accessed 18 February 2024.
33. 'Dutch Childcare Benefits scandal 2021' Wikipedia, available at https://en.wikipedia.org/wiki/Dutch_childcare_benefits_scandal, accessed 18 February 2024.
34. G. Geiger, 'How Denmark's Welfare State Became a Surveillance Nightmare', Wired, 07 March 2023, available at https://www.wired.com/story/algorithms-welfare-state-politics/, accessed 18 February 2024.

ARTICLE

Finding My Sparkle: When Recordkeeping Practitioner and Research Life Intertwine to Become One

Catherine Victoria Nicholls*

Records Manager, Information and Records Management, Monash University, Melbourne, Australia

Abstract

This article discusses the interplay between recordkeeping research and practice through the author's experiences as both a part time researcher and full-time practitioner. By drawing on narrative inquiry in the form of autoethnography, the author uses their current research project as a catalyst for exploring the relationship between practitioner life and research work. Their research project investigates how family recordkeeping can be utilised to provide an entry point into understanding recordkeeping concepts and practices in the workplace. The paper explores how the author's research activities were initially considered secondary and separate from their practitioner life. As the project progressed, their practices helped to shape elements of the research design; and later, the research data played a key role in helping the author to frame the role of recordkeeping literacy in their work program. The author developed a new confidence as they used different analysis tools including scrapbooking and podcasting which in turn brought real enjoyment to the project, a joy that later spilled over and invigorated their practitioner life. Overall, it has become apparent to the author that a recordkeeping career does not need to be a binary proposition between academia or practitioner life.

Keywords: *Research*; *Practitioner experience*; *Family Recordkeeping*; *Autoethnography*

In a sun-kissed room, in the outer suburbs of Melbourne, a large pile of children's artwork is roughly divided into a number of different stacks. Some of it has spilled out from underneath one of the chairs, while more pieces lay spread across the living room coffee table. The mother of the young children indicates that the many pieces of artwork have just become part of the 'savannah of daily life' in the home. Yet, some pieces of artwork have made their way onto the loungeroom wall, affixed with sticky tape, and others are magnetised to the fridge in the kitchen. Another piece has been framed and proudly resides in the home's hallway.

At first glance, this description seems far removed from the realities of workplace recordkeeping, yet on closer examination there is much to explore. The children's artwork from this

*Correspondence: Catherine Victoria Nicholls Email: catherine.nicholls@monash.edu

loungeroom in outer Melbourne all form part of this family's recordkeeping story, which is also a key part of my current research work into family recordkeeping.

In this article, I discuss the interplay between recordkeeping research and practice throughout my experiences as both a part time researcher and full-time practitioner over a 27 year plus recordkeeping career. Undertaking research activities has been a constant theme across my practitioner life. Up until recently, I believed that I pursued extra-curricular study with research components because I enjoyed the challenge of learning new things. I have never aspired to become a full-time researcher or academic in my field nor have I widely published. In a way, undertaking small-scale research and study projects felt like they had very little to do with my practitioner life. I will outline my own story as a practitioner but I will draw upon my most current research activities into family recordkeeping to explore how I have come to understand that research and practitioner life can become firmly intertwined, complementing each other in ways I have only recently come to appreciate.

Narrative inquiry

The concepts of narrative inquiry and autoethnography provide important context for both the tone and shape of this article and how I present my work. Narrative enquiry has become core to my research work. It influences the way in which I undertake research, and informs how I reflect on and think about my practitioner and research work and the relationships between the two.

Jane Elliott notes that:

> a narrative can be understood to organise a sequence of events into a whole so that the significance of each event can be understood through its relation to the whole. In this way a narrative conveys the meaning of events.[1]

Narrative inquiry provides a structure for the exploration of complex matters in a way that makes sense to me.[2] As someone who is less comfortable around spreadsheets and sets of figures, I appreciate the warmth and liveliness of the stories held within my research data. The process of bringing those stories to light makes the analysis process more in-depth and engaging than other research methods. Narrative inquiry can be utilised to harness personal expression and reflection in multiple creative ways, within the framework of a rigorous set of proven research steps and processes.[3]

Autoethnography can be described as a form of 'autobiographical narrative inquiry'[4] that presents 'critical self-study'[5] as research. It encourages the rigorous examination of personal experience within the context of a project's research questions. For my current research project, I have situated my use of autoethnography within a broader narrative enquiry framework. The use of autoethnography as a way of framing research is not an uncommon theme in recordkeeping literature. Joanne Evans speaks of autoethnography as a mechanism for reflecting on how her role as a practitioner has influenced her research, bringing her practitioner experience out of the shadows and allowing it to be framed within her research work.[6] Evans also touches upon how autoethnography provides a means to explore and highlight the 'insider' versus 'outsider' role of the researcher and practitioner.

This insider/outsider contrast is further explored through the work of Belinda Battley, who also discusses the value of autoethnography. Battley talks about the process of blogging as part of how she manages 'the three wired bridge',[7] a metaphor that sums up the many hats Battley wore as a researcher, participant and friend of the communities she was researching. For Evans and Battley, autoethnography provides an opportunity to monitor and reflect on their various roles and the different 'hats' worn at different stages of their research. It validates their research approach and adds valuable insights into their overall results. I am still exploring how I use autoethnography within the context of narrative inquiry in my current research project. However, for the purposes of this article, I am utilising autoethnography in a way similar to Evans: as a mechanism to reflect on how my practitioner life has ended up shaping my research, as well as how my research data influenced my work program in an Australian tertiary institution.

Career background
Following undergraduate studies in history, I studied for my Masters of Information Management and Systems at Monash University (Australia) during the 1990s. While studying, I entered the profession and began my career in recordkeeping. At that early stage of my career I did not fully appreciate the theoretical frameworks we were introduced to, including the newly minted Records Continuum Model.[8] Instead, I was more concerned about learning the practicalities of my first job in a tertiary archives program. I suspect it was around this time that I subconsciously separated my academic understanding of the field from what I was doing in my day-to-day work life. It is also likely that this is where my perception that academic research and practitioner life were quite separate activities took hold.

A 2012 article by Elizabeth Shepherd provides some reassuring context for this perceived separation of activities. Shepherd documented the historical 'dilemma' the recordkeeping field has with its own identity as both a profession and an academic discipline.[9] Although Shepherd was writing about the profession from the UK perspective, she noted that the 1990s were when the 'foundations of the modern [recordkeeping] academic discipline were being laid down'.[10] Although I did not recognise it at the time, the same foundations were being laid down in an Australian recordkeeping academic life.

Others have also hinted at some non-cohesive elements within the wider field. Anne Gilliland and Sue McKemmish have stressed that recordkeeping needs its academic discipline and practice elements to both bring 'identifiable, distinctive and rigorous perspectives and toolsets of methods and techniques'.[11] In 2022, Alex Poole and Ashley Todd-Diaz explored a number of pressing issues facing archival education in North America via case study and interview. In this recent study, the historical tensions between academia and practice in recordkeeping are still evident, for example in the comment that 'the scholarly audience tends to be just a little turned off by the issues that interest professionals'.[12] I agree with this statement and suggest that it could potentially be reversed to recognise that professionals are sometimes not engaged with some of the issues that interest scholars.

Although I was never 'turned off' by the issues or themes taught to me in my Masters course, I recall struggling to relate what I had been taught to the challenges of my first professional job. I did not really comprehend for example, how the Records Continuum Model would help me to perfect my box folding skills or teach me the basics of archive repository management.

Over time though, as my career progressed into more senior-level recordkeeping roles, I came to better appreciate what I had learnt through that first degree and I started incorporating aspects of it into my practitioner life. In particular, I would return to the learnings from that course to help contextualise some of the challenges I was seeing in my practitioner role, especially those presented by electronic recordkeeping. Although outside the scope of this article, I also came to better appreciate the role and purpose of the Records Continuum Model as I advanced in my practitioner career, and later when I started to explore my research interests.

As I continued to undertake study and research during the middle stages of my career, I became aware that I was pursuing my own academic interests for enjoyment. For example, around 2010, I delved into the field of Early Childhood Education (ECE), which at that stage, had no connection at all to my senior records manager role in an Australian tertiary institution. It was through my current research project that I started making more connections between my research and practitioner life. I will now turn to this research project and explain in more detail how the project and my practitioner life have developed alongside each other.

The current research project

I came into the topic of family recordkeeping around children through an ECE focus. Initially I had not considered that the ECE component of my study interests would ever intersect with my recordkeeping practitioner life. As I went further into my studies in ECE, I completed a research project on the role of government policy and the Australian Children's Television Standards. From there, I started to develop an interest in ECE curriculum policy.

After completing ECE studies, I was thinking about my next research project and was looking to pursue my PhD in the Faculty of Education at Monash University. At this stage, I was introduced to the aptly titled 'Early Years Learning Framework – Belonging, Being & Becoming ECE policy document'.[13] This framework focuses on the delivery of multiple learning outcomes across the early childhood curriculum, including teaching children key themes such as identity, understanding one's place in the world and the value of communication.

I have previously written about the role of records and recordkeeping processes in determining identity and how individuals connected to each other.[14] As Cook notes:

> beyond evidence, archives also preserve memory ... archives are constructed memories of the past, about history, heritage, and culture, about personal roots and familial connections, and about who we are as human beings ... memory and forgetting, can serve a whole range of practical, cultural, political, symbolic, emotional and ethical imperatives and is central to power, identity and privilege.[15]

Originally, when the research problem was framed within an ECE setting, my focus was on establishing why the role of recordkeeping in people's lives was rarely perceived as a topic of mainstream interest outside the world of professional records managers and archivists. An overview of the existing literature in this space has also been documented in a previous article.[16]

My literature review for the research project revealed a mismatch between the perception of records management in the workplace and the role that recordkeeping played in people's personal lives. The former could be seen as a boring 'tick box' compliance activity compared to the more thought-provoking, intriguing nature of personal recordkeeping. However, though corporate records management had been written about and researched throughout the recordkeeping literature, there was less focus on what McKemmish describes as the role of 'personal recordkeeping cultures'.[17] I wondered if there was evidence to suggest that personal recordkeeping had a role to play in creating a sense of belonging, especially for children and families.

My original multidisciplinary doctoral research project therefore aimed to investigate family records and recordkeeping practices in order to understand the role of recordkeeping in children's early years learning and development. I determined that the best methodology would be to interview a small number of parents about the recordkeeping activities they undertook around their children within the home. In brief, the research design for this research project included a literature review, a series of interviews with five parents who had at least one child aged between 0 and 8 years old at the time of the interview, a focus group with five workplace colleagues (to validate the findings from the interviews) and associated analysis and write ups of the findings.

Family recordkeeping interviews

I chose to interview five parents in order to gain a broad, but not overwhelming, number of different types of family recordkeeping for the study. The initial participants were drawn from people in my own professional acquaintance circle, which at that point included people I had met through work, study or through professional networks. It is important to acknowledge that the selection of participants for this study was representative of people encountered in my work at an Australian University. This is a socio-economically privileged environment where most participants have had the opportunity to engage in tertiary-level education or participate in the tertiary sector workforce.

I was therefore aware that the participants were not going to be representative of the wider Australian community as a whole. The decision to include families who had a connection to tertiary education was not consciously embedded into the research design of the project at the beginning. As the research project evolved and my own life and work experiences began to influence the study, it became apparent that focusing on research participants who also form part of my practitioner world was going to become more pertinent.

My interview questions for the family recordkeeping interviews were semi-structured (focusing on particular themes and concepts, but without relying solely on fixed questions to provide scope for exploring ideas and responses as they emerged). I approached the development of the interview questions from a functional recordkeeping perspective.[18] The questions that were developed for the family interviews were framed around an understanding of the key functions that take place within a typical family. As far as I was aware there were no established, published sets of functions developed for recordkeeping analysis within families. This would make sense as these tools were originally developed for use in government agency settings.[19]

When thinking about the key family functions that could be used to classify different types of recordkeeping activities I considered my own experiences growing up in a family, as well as typical functions that may also take place within the homes of friends and family. I also consulted the Australian Early Development Census[20]; however, the Census data was classified for statistical purposes which was not helpful when thinking about family functions from a recordkeeping perspective. I therefore created my own set of family functions which are included further in the text. I have also noted some of the activities and records that might sit underneath each of the following functions.

- **Family Celebrations** (e.g. demonstrated through activities such as birthday parties, and creating records such invitations and birthday cards)
- **Family Health and Wellbeing** (e.g. demonstrated through activities such as doctor visits, immunisations, medical diagnosis and creating records such as 'baby' birth books, immunisation records, birth charts, etc.)
- **Children's Education** (e.g. demonstrated through activities such as attending day care, kindergarten or school and creating records such as school reports, photographs and artwork, etc.)

Why functions?

My background practitioner experience led me to use functions as a guide when structuring the research interviews. As a practitioner I was aware of the limitations in taking a function-based approach to a recordkeeping consultation with work colleagues. For example, there is always the risk that you might end up over-structuring the interview and miss important recordkeeping activities as the interviewee may feel that they can only speak to the 'prescribed' functions. On the other side, I have also experienced how asking people to talk about their records and recordkeeping activities without any functional context can lead to blank looks and a fair amount of confusion. For example, questions such as 'tell me about your recordkeeping activities' make too many assumptions about an audiences' level of recordkeeping literacy and provide limited entry points into the conversation. Instead, using functions and associated activity-based examples of recordkeeping as an entry point to a broader discussion around recordkeeping is usually quite effective. I have found this approach helpful for consultations at work, and so decided to use it to interview participants in the home environment about their family recordkeeping activities.

Prior to the interviews, some of the participants indicated that they were unsure if they created any records at home within the family. I introduced the family functions and examples into the interview questions, which prompted the interviewees to start thinking about their family recordkeeping activities. For example, in many cases the parent spoke about birthday celebrations and the recordkeeping associated with that activity. This then led them to other topics, such as how they managed photographs and activities associated with social media.

Initial responses to the interview results

The interviews with the five participating parents were conducted from May to August 2017. During this process, the importance of individual recordkeeping values and behaviours in families started to emerge as a theme. For example, several of the participants self-identified as 'someone who doesn't like to throw things away', while others declared they were more attached to a 'minimalist' house aesthetic. For this second group, throwing things away when they were no longer needed (including children's artwork for example) was seen as completely necessary. In this early stage of the analysis I recognised that my study was small, and that perhaps I was reading too much into my participants self-described personality traits. On reflection however it appeared to me that the decision to keep a room neat or tidy, or the choice of a minimalist decorating style at home did reflect an individual's overall values and behaviours; and within that, such values and behaviours were influencing the recordkeeping activities that were taking place within the home.

In my work I had thought about the roles and behaviours that could be present within an organisation or work team; however, I had not considered how such values and behaviours might originate and play out on an individual level. While it would be hard to measure exactly how much one individual's recordkeeping values and behaviours might hold sway across a large work team or organisation, understanding that this element will be in the mix, provides a more nuanced understanding when thinking about my own practitioner experiences.

Often, when providing recordkeeping advice in an organisational setting, my focus was on improving a business process or improving the evidentiary value of the record. It could then come as a shock if that advice (which felt neutral at the time of delivery) was met with emotional resistance or opposition. My first reaction to such a response was to think that perhaps there is not enough stakeholder 'buy in' or that there was a resourcing issue – all of which might have been true. However, the family recordkeeping project demonstrated to me just how closely an individual's values and behaviours are entwined with recordkeeping activities, and that this can provoke quite strong emotional responses when challenged. This has led me to ask more questions and undertake a closer analysis in my practitioner life, especially when it comes to working with groups or even individuals who are implementing new recordkeeping processes or activities.

I also turned to the literature to see what had been documented about the role of values and behaviours in personal recordkeeping, starting with the information culture research work by Gillian Oliver and Fiorella Foscarini. Interestingly, they did not have a lot to say about information culture on the home front. Oliver and Foscarini note their focus is on organisational recordkeeping values and behaviours, while recognising:

an interesting avenue for future research in the records management context: being able to associate specific behaviour types with the different layers of culture will provide us with significant insight. For instance, one may assume that appraising records and assigning retention periods will partly reflect value systems acquired through the family, the social context one grew up in, and later through school; while the activities involved in registering records and routing them to specific employees will be primarily influenced by workplace practices and professional skills.[21]

This led me to question why the traditional forms of workplace recordkeeping training in my field often fell short of delivering the expected outcomes. Once again, I relied on my practitioner experience to help me think more deeply about what I was observing. I was used to providing two key types of recordkeeping training. One type focused on explaining the terms used in recordkeeping (e.g. 'what is a record'?) and outlining the legal obligations and compliance issues around recordkeeping; and the other was more focused on how to use an electronic document and records management system to capture and manage records. In both cases, I observed that the initial enthusiasm for undertaking the recordkeeping task that led a participant to undertake the training in the first place would fade once the training was complete. Often, I would then see the same people coming back asking the same recordkeeping questions. I could see that this type of traditional recordkeeping training was disconnected from what my colleagues were dealing with on the ground. They were not always willing or able to apply the recordkeeping rules, regulations and systems training to manage a shared drive, or to decide what system to use when storing important records. This is perhaps further exacerbated by the sheer scale and size of the information management landscape in the large-scale tertiary institution where I currently work. As with any complex institution there are often many options, processes and systems (potentially hundreds) working in tandem at any one point in time. While the overarching rules and regulations have a role to play, there also need to be other layers and access points to allow the various groups working across the organisation to relate these broader information management or recordkeeping principles to their day-to-day activities.

This reflection led me to question whether these traditional forms of workplace recordkeeping training addressed the right things. I wondered (along with my supervisors of my PhD) if there was a gap in terms of the types of recordkeeping training I was used to providing. Perhaps the gap was the false assumption that all non-recordkeeping practitioners had a certain level of recordkeeping literacy.

As a practitioner and a researcher, these questions eventually led me to explore whether my research into family recordkeeping could be utilised to provide an entry point into recordkeeping literacy and fluency that could generate more meaningful and accessible understandings of recordkeeping concepts and practices in the workplace. I needed an approach that incorporated recordkeeping values and behaviours, rather than just a focus on records management rules and regulations. In combination with other factors (including an unforeseen health situation, explained in the final section of this paper) my practitioner-led realisation about workplace recordkeeping literacy eventually led to a change in the whole structure of my PhD. By 2023, my research was no longer in the field of Education and I had transferred into the records and archives domain in the Faculty of Information Technology, with a renewed focus on the role of family recordkeeping in designing workplace recordkeeping literacy.

Analysis process – scrapbooking
Analysis of the family recordkeeping interview data occurred over a long period of time.

The research data was full of small anecdotes and beautiful stories that I wanted to keep alive; I did not want to risk losing some of its vibrancy by reducing it to a set of words sitting in tables and spreadsheets. While many find coding data an effective approach for seeking patterns and insights, it was not aligned with how I was making sense of the family recordkeeping interview data. My overall process was also influenced by narrative inquiry methodology. Reissman notes that 'just as interview participants tell stories, investigators construct stories from their data'.[22] She goes on to discuss how narrative can be represented visually, supported by examples including where researchers have retold their data stories via stain glass windows, cinema and even comics.

I chose to undertake my analysis stage through the creation of scrapbooks that visually represented key points from each of the interview transcripts. In summary, I would begin by re-reading the transcript from each interview to re-familiarise myself with the family and the contents of the interview. Then I would start to break down the interview transcript into sections. I would print out the transcript and use brightly coloured pens to make little annotations in the margins about the stories that were popping out from the text. These were not meant to be detailed notes, but rather points of interest that stood out to me from the interviews. As I was using the scrapbooks to re-story the interview transcripts, I thought about what I wanted to represent visually and how this would be achieved.

Each family recordkeeping interview was roughly represented across 12–20 individual pages within two scrapbook albums. Families 1, 2 and the first part of Family 3 are represented in the first scrapbook album, and the second part of Family 3, all of Families 5 and 6 are in the second scrapbook album. Each page of the scrapbook albums contains a double-sided page sitting within a plastic sleeve. Each page of these scrapbook albums represented one section of one of the family recordkeeping transcripts. There is one section of a transcript from one family on the front side and another section on the back of each scrapbook album page. Each page has been constructed using a combination of my own hand drawn illustrations, store bought scrapbooking paper, papercraft decorations, stickers and stencils.

The advantage of using a scrapbook album was that they came with specially designed sleeves. This meant that the scrapbook album pages could be easily removed (by simply opening the clip binding) and placed into different orders, which became useful when I was looking across the albums for common themes, as represented via the family functions.

The detail on each scrapbook album page was constructed using a combination of my own hand drawn illustrations, store bought scrapbooking paper, papercraft decorations, stickers and stencils. Rather than transcribe the interviews word for word, I created visual cues or symbols to help retell the recordkeeping story from the parent's point of view. In Figure 1, a mother tells a story of going to a doctor's appointment and recalls her newborn's 'baby book' record falling from the stroller and being run over by a car. She was able to retrieve the book, but she recalls the medical professional being somewhat surprised and judgemental by the book's condition when she eventually made it into the appointment.

While the end product is quite simple, the analysis was enriched by my process of thinking of how best to visually represent the different recordkeeping stories each section of the scrapbook album aims to tell.

In many ways, this was a really enjoyable experience as I have always taken on craft projects in my personal life. I soon realised that by undertaking the analysis in this way, I was constantly thinking about the transcripts during the creation of each scrapbook page. Little subtleties such as a turn of phrase from the interview subject, or a small anecdote would come to life and lead me to think deeply about what that particular content told me about my research topic. As I scoured sections of the transcript to create each scrapbook album page, certain

Figure 1. Example of scrapbooking folders, photograph taken by author.

stories from the research interviews would become embedded in my thoughts. This process prevented me from skipping over things and potentially missing important details that I may not have picked up otherwise. This approach to analysis resonated and made sense to me, even though at times it felt quite unorthodox, and not like a 'serious' or 'formal' way of doing research. However, as my supervisors explained to me, it was a rigorous process and I could document each step, so it met the criteria of research analysis. This improved my confidence as both a researcher and practitioner. It helped me to realise that my ideas were valid and I could use practices and ways of undertaking research that made sense to me, even if they didn't feel overly 'academic'.

Significance of the family recordkeeping findings
When thinking about the significance of the interview findings, it became apparent that many of the issues being discussed in the family recordkeeping space, including which record was the authoritative one and what option was best when it came to storage, were also present in my practitioner life. In the workplace, for example, I would often observe that the plethora of digital information systems on offer, with their many parts containing multiple versions of data, meant many non-recordkeeping trained colleagues would encounter understandable difficulties determining what was in fact the authoritative record. For example, was the email in which the information was transmitted the authoritative record, or was the record in the system where the information was processed the authority? Lacking the understanding required to easily identify the authoritative record would sometimes lead to other recordkeeping challenges, such as the over retention of records, or the proliferation of records across multiple storage locations.

I witnessed this behaviour of wanting to keep similar types of records together even if that meant creating duplicates both in the workplace and the family recordkeeping examples. Identifying and making decisions about where and how long to store externally issued records (e.g. passports, vaccination status records, etc), was also a common topic across the workplace environment. This led me to think about the design of the final research gathering exercise for the project. I settled on validating my family recordkeeping interview findings with a focus group of work colleagues. My hypothesis was that thinking about recordkeeping behaviours and values in one's personal life was a potential entry point as a first step into developing base level workplace recordkeeping literacy skills.

Validating the family recordkeeping results
I presented the family recordkeeping interview findings to the focus group of work colleagues in October 2023, alongside three fairly common workplace recordkeeping questions:

- What is an authoritative record?
- Where should records be stored?
- What is the value of recordkeeping?

The 1-h focus group was run online. Before attending, the participants were asked to listen to a pre-recorded podcast. As the focus group would involve five work colleagues, who I knew were already busy, I thought that listening to a podcast as part of the focus group preparation was an easier proposition than presenting them with pages of reading material. The podcast enabled the focus group participants to listen to the findings from the family recordkeeping stories at their own pace and in their preferred environment.

In preparing these podcasts I had to think carefully about how to use some of the quotes from the transcripts, and whether I should use music. In the end, I created a script and worked on using different kinds of tones with my voice to indicate when I was sharing a story using the words of my interview participants. I also purchased some music to use for the introduction and conclusion sections of the podcast. Making editing decisions for the final version of the podcast was at times a slightly frustrating and fiddly endeavour, but one which I ultimately really enjoyed and learnt a number of new skills from. The focus group provided a range of useful insights to the research project overall, as well as validating a number of key observations made during the family recordkeeping interviews. At the time of writing, the final analysis of this work and write up of the research is in progress.

When life gets in the way …
Towards the end of the family recordkeeping interview stage of the research project, a number of changes in my life started to occur which impacted both the direction and focus of the research project, my practitioner world and my life overall.

Around early 2018 I had become quite ill. Although I was able to recover, I was left with significant long-term health issues. This explains the break away from the research project and why there is such a gap between the data gathering stage (2017) and the focus group stage (2023). Overall, I took approximately three and a half years of leave from the thesis in order to focus on my health. I only resumed the research work again at the beginning of 2023.

When I first had to step away from the research, I was dismayed. I also was not sure if I was ever going to be able to go back to it. At that initial discontinuation point I assumed there was nothing more I could do. Gradually my health improved and I started to notice that I was still drawing on the findings from the family recordkeeping interviews in my practitioner role. I was regularly thinking about the value of the interviews and how those parents were able to effortlessly demonstrate their acquired recordkeeping knowledge, even though their self-assessment of that knowledge was quite low at the beginning of the interviews.

During the hiatus period I also recognised that the parents involved in the study were not following any government recordkeeping rules or policies when it came to managing their children's records at home. This makes sense, as no such rules or policies exist in the family setting. Yet, when they spoke about their various family functions, it became apparent that all of the parents were capturing, controlling, accessing, storing, disposing of or preserving records as part of their day-to-day lives. I found significant evidence of recordkeeping activities being undertaken, even if the parents themselves did not identify them as related to 'recordkeeping'.

Often, they described these activities as 'life admin', or 'memory making' tasks. With my practitioner hat on, I realised that by exclusively focusing on recordkeeping policy and processes as the foundational content for recordkeeping training, I was making too many assumptions about the recordkeeping literacy level of my audience. Perhaps my practitioner hypothesis was on the right track. I was also reminded through the research that most people can easily relate to recordkeeping practices when seen through the lens of personal recordkeeping. I went back to the work of Oliver and Foscarini[23] and the idea of workplace recordkeeping behaviours and values. General discussions with my team at work at this time based on the family recordkeeping findings led to a number of changes in how we shared recordkeeping information with our organisational colleagues. This included how we explained recordkeeping concepts and how we thought about training programs, as well as influencing the professional terms we used (or in some cases deliberately stopped using with certain audiences).

After realising how much the original family recordkeeping research data was still influencing my practitioner role, I wanted to understand why these findings felt so important and relevant, especially in relation to workplace recordkeeping training. I realised that I needed to go back to the research and explore my findings in more detail. I suspected some of the answers to my questions might come through applying records continuum theory to the problem; however, I was aware that I would need some guidance. This was one of the key drivers behind my return to formal study.

My enforced 'pause' could be characterised as 'laying fallow'. As Friedman and Yoo state:

> this form of pause serves the purpose of refreshing people, resources, or other aspects of the project. Such fallow periods aid with project sustainability and can act as a counterpoint to what might be experienced as relentless project workflow leading to burnout.[24]

With hindsight, my health situation allowed me to take on the 'design mechanism of pause' – an unexpected but positive outcome to becoming so ill.

Conclusion

My overriding belief now is that research enriches my practitioner life. While timing, resources, life circumstances and the right research opportunity all play a role in determining how much research can be incorporated into a practitioner role, it should never be perceived as an either/or situation. This binary notion of practitioner versus researcher is now no longer part of my subconscious or conscious mindset.

The joy that narrative inquiry has brought to my current research project into family recordkeeping cannot be underestimated. This method has encouraged me to take a creative approach towards my research process, including capturing stories during my family recordkeeping interviews, and re-storying those experiences back into scrapbooking as part of my analysis. It has also enabled me to draw upon narrative methodology techniques to present my data in different ways, including creating a podcast full of short stories for my focus group exercise. The ability to design a research project based around how I see and understand the world has made the research journey infinitely more enjoyable and rewarding for me as both a researcher and practitioner in the recordkeeping field. My research has enabled me to share my theoretical findings and insights with my work program team and colleagues, and the ability to provide a sound rationale as a practitioner has helped to remove some of the guesswork out of planning and strategic thinking exercises across our activities and program as a whole.

On a personal level, the research has improved my writing skills and my conceptual thinking. It has also provided me with invaluable and exciting insights into how I view the world and take in and process complex information. The discovery of the narrative theory, and the use of autoethnography within that approach, has validated my natural instincts to want to represent both my research and practitioner life creatively in order to make sense of it. I came across the idea of scrapbooking through this research project because it ultimately made the most sense to me in terms of an analysis technique. What I did not realise until recently was that using hand drawn pictures and paper craft is a really valuable way for me to make sense of the world more generally, well beyond my work and study life.

My personal journaling activities now include small components of papercraft/scrapbooking exercises as a way to process and make sense of my current health journey as well as day to day life. I employed this process during my laying fallow period on the thesis to keep myself connected to the research when I was so unwell. Even during the worst of the illness, I would still complete a few scrapbook pages across weeks, and sometimes months, in order to stay connected to my data. However, this also helped me to process the findings and think about their relevance to my work program. Writing things down does not, on its own, provide a useful way for me to engage with new thinking or problem solving. Now, through the narrative inquiry methodology, I have found a way to help make better sense of both my research problems, and my practitioner life and beyond.

I can't recommend the bringing together of research into a practitioner role highly enough. No matter the scale, be it large or small, undertaking research and incorporating it into my practitioner life has been and continues to be one of the most rewarding and long-lasting aspects of my career in recordkeeping. It has been and continues to be a key source of my sparkle!

Notes on contributor

Catherine started her career in the Monash University Archives, while she also completed her Masters of Information Management & Systems (Hons) with a thesis component that explored the role of exhibitions in archive outreach programs. Catherine later moved to the University of Melbourne for 10 years in a series of practitioner roles including Manager, Records Services. During this time, Catherine also completed her Masters of Education (Early Childhood Education) with a research component that focused on the Australian Children's Television Standards. In 2011, Catherine took on the role of Records Manager at Monash University and in 2023 recommenced her PhD studies, also at Monash University in the Faculty of Information Technology.

Acknowledgements

I would like to thank my current PhD supervisors, Associate Professor Joanne Evans and Dr Greg Rolan for their ongoing support with the research project discussed in this article, and also for their insightful feedback suggestions with the construction of this paper. The initial structure of the research project, in particular the family recordkeeping interviews owes much to both Associate Professor Joanne Evans as well as Dr Jane Bone.

Notes

1. J Elliott, Using Narrative in Social Research: Qualitative and Quantitative Approaches (1st ed., pp. xi–xi). Sage, London, 2005, p. 3.
2. K Jeong-Hee, Understanding Narrative Inquiry: The Crafting and Analysis of Stories as Research, Sage, Thousand Oaks, CA, 2016.
3. ibid.
4. ibid., p. 121.
5. ibid., p. 123.
6. J Evans, 'Designing Dynamic Descriptive Frameworks', Archives and Manuscripts, vol. 42, no. 1, 2014, p. 7.
7. B Battley, 'Co-producing Archival Research with Communication, Reflexivity and Friendship: Crossing the Three-wire Bridge', Archival Science, vol. 17, no. 4, 2017, pp. 371–391.
8. F Upward, 'Modelling the Continuum as Paradigm Shift in Recordkeeping and Archiving Processes, and Beyond: A Personal Reflection', Records Management Journal, vol. 10, no. 3, 2000, pp. 115–139.
9. E Shepherd, 'An "Academic" Dilemma: The Tale of Archives and Records Management', Journal of Librarianship and Information Science, vol. 44, no. 3, 2012, pp. 174–184.
10. ibid., p. 175.
11. A Gilliland and S McKemmish, 'Building an Infrastructure for Archival Research', Archival Science, vol. 4, no. 3–4, 2004, p. 154.
12. AH Poole and A Todd-Diaz, '"I'm Not a Very Good Visionary": Challenge and Change in Twenty-First Century North American Archival Education', Archival Science, vol. 22, no. 4, 2022, p. 597.
13. Department of Education, Employment and Workplace Relations DEEWR. Belonging, Being & Becoming – The Early Years Learning Framework for Australia, Commonwealth of Australia, Canberra, 2009.
14. C Nicholls, 'Making the Case for Recordkeeping Literacy: A Narrative Approach', Archives and Manuscripts, vol. 46, no. 2, 2018, pp. 143–157.
15. T Cook, 'Evidence, Memory, Identity and Community: Four Shifting Archival Paradigms', Archival Science, vol. 13, no. 2, 2013, p. 101.
16. Nicholls, 2018.
17. S McKemmish, ''Evidence of Me', The Australian Library Journal, vol. 45, no. 3, 1996, p. 175.
18. See National Archives of Australia, Types of Records Authorities, available at https://www.naa.gov.au/information-management/records-authorities/types-records-authorities, accessed 21 October, 2023, for examples of how some typical government type functions.
19. C Hurley, 'What, If Anything, Is a Function?', Archives and Manuscripts, vol. 21, no. 2, 1993, pp. 208–220.
20. See Australian Early Development Census: An Australian Government Initiative, available at https://www.aedc.gov.au/, accessed 21 October, 2023, as an example of how the Federal Government breaks down different activities for reporting purposes. There was nothing specific about this resource that provided guidance for developing my family functions, however it was still a useful resource to review to see how language was used to classify family life and early childhood development.
21. G Oliver and F Foscarini, Records Management and Information Culture: Tackling the People Problem, Facet Publishing, London, 2014, p. 37.
22. CK Riessman, Narrative Methods for the Human Sciences, Sage, Thousand Oaks, CA, 2008, p. 4.
23. Oliver and Foscarini, 2014.
24. B Friedman and D Yoo, 'Pause: A Multi-lifespan Design Mechanism', in Proceedings of the 2017 CHI Conference on Human Factors in Computing Systems (CHI'17), Association for Computing Machinery, New York, 6–11 May 2017, p. 462.

REFLECTION
Post-Custodialism, Distributed Custody, and Big Data

James Doig*

Digital Preservation Manager, National Archives of Australia, Canberra, Australian Capital Territory

Abstract

This reflection piece describes the outcomes of a research project undertaken by the National Archives of Australia that aimed to gather information from other government archives and selected Australian government agencies about their approach to archiving and preserving large-big datasets in the government sector. Big data collections pose a challenge for government archives around the world. Many of these archives have a role in information management in their government domains and provide guidance and advice to their government agency clients on ensuring the integrity and trustworthiness of data over time. The article examines the nexus between theory and practice, exploring issues related to the post-custodial ideas developed by Terry Cook and others in the 1990s and their practical implementation.

Keywords: *Distributed custody*; *Post-custodialism*; *Digital preservation*; *Big data*

This article reflects on the results of a research project carried out by the National Archives of Australia (NAA) in 2022 on large and big data producing agencies (i.e. in the high terabyte and petabyte size) and the challenges posed by big data collections to archives. By telling the story, I want to highlight the important work accomplished in the 1990s and early 2000s regarding recordkeeping standards and guidance – work that involved close collaboration between theorists and practitioners who espoused post-custodial approaches to archival and records management. Much of this work, especially around distributed custody, appears to have been forgotten, and it is worth drawing attention to it again in the context of big data.

Theory and practice in the 1990s

The second half of the 1990s is surely the high-water mark in collaboration between theorists and practitioners in Australia. In particular, the records continuum model developed at Monash University by Frank Upward and others influenced the development of foundational standards, policy guidance, and advice on recordkeeping and information management. Theorists and practitioners participated in the development of the world-first records management standard, AS 4390. Released by Standards Australia in 1996, it was the starting point for the

*Correspondence: James Doig, Email: james.doig@naa.gov.au

International Standards Organization's 2001 standard on records management, ISO 15489.[1] National Archives developed the 'e-permanence' suite of advisory products that Commonwealth government agencies could use to build best practice recordkeeping environments.[2] The cornerstone of e-permanence, released in 2000, was the *Designing and Implementing Recordkeeping Systems (DIRKS) Manual*.[3] A joint development of the State Records Authority (RA) of New South Wales and the National Archives, the DIRKS Manual built on AS 4390 to provide comprehensive practical guidance on designing and implementing a recordkeeping system via an eight-step methodology that was included in outline in AS 4390 and which heralded the brave new world of functions-based appraisal.[4]

e-permanence was itself heavily influenced by the post-custodial theory that had informed the continuum model and that was most eloquently championed by the Canadian archivist and theorist, Terry Cook. Cook gave an invitational lecture tour of Australia in 1993 (see Figure 1) and his seminal article published the following year, 'Electronic Records, Paper Minds: The Revolution in Information Management and Archives in the Post-Custodial and Post-Modernist Era', was based on a lecture he delivered several times during his tour.[5]

When the National Archives implemented a distributed custody policy for digital records in 1996, the policy intent was succinctly expressed as follows: 'the preferred arrangement is for agencies to retain custody of electronic records of ongoing value, but under a management regime worked out with the Australian Archives'.[6] The standards, policy guidance, and advice developed often in close partnership with theorists constituted the management regime. Although the development of a digital preservation capability brought an end to the distributed custody policy after 4 years, the management frameworks for post-custodialism and distributed custody were in place by the turn of the millennium and are still with us today, though the tools have continued to evolve.

This period also saw the development of practical rules for the management of digital records subject to distributed custody arrangements. As early as 1993, the National Archives of Canada had policies and rules for distributed custody in place, including a clear articulation of the circumstances in which archival value digital records would be left with the creating government institution. These were listed by Terry Cook in a 1995 article:

1. Where the cost of transfer of the record or other technical considerations (software copyright, data complexity, software and hardware dependency, etc.) make it impossible for the Archives to acquire the record at this time and/or
2. Where the institution has a continuing and long-term operational need for the record, which includes the provision of elaborate and extensive reference services and/or
3. Where because of the nature of the record reference services can best be provided by the institution rather than by the Archives and/or
4. Where there are statutory provisions that prevent transfer to the Archives.[7]

Interestingly, the main categories of records identified as candidates for distributed custody quite closely reflect the current big data environment in government, including cumulative and longitudinal systems such as scientific, environmental, and social data. Some of the terms and conditions developed by the Canadians also remain relevant today. For example, the National Archives may exercise the right to transfer the records into custody if there are major systems changes or where systems are to be decommissioned. That said, the preservation requirements reflect a period when information tended to be stored on 9-track magnetic tape in off-line storage environments[8], and where Cook was talking about reference services involving people, in particular telephone inquiry services, these days agencies like the Bureau of Meteorology

Figure 1. Terry Cook [centre, with Mark Stevens and Ann Pederson] visits Australia, State Library of New South Wales, Macquarie Street Sydney, 1993. Image courtesy of City of Sydney Archives: A-00028118.

(BOM), Geoscience, and the Australian Bureau of Statistics (ABS) provide sophisticated online access to their data.

Digital preservation theory and practice have developed enormously since the mid-1990s, but the now well-known digital preservation principles and approaches – multiple independent storage, integrity checking, migration strategies, and so on – impose a hefty cost for petabyte size data and may be a barrier to distributed custody agreements with agencies.

Big data project

The National Archives' research project, conducted in 2022, was a response to issues raised by government agencies that are creating and managing large-big datasets. This includes agencies managing massive datasets in single systems (for example, BOM) and agencies with data assets distributed across many medium-sized systems (for example, ABS). In particular, the following three key business problems were identified:

1. *Information management challenges:* applying information management standards and requirements, particularly disposal requirements, to large-big datasets can be a challenge for agencies.
2. *Transfer, preservation, and access:* under the *Archives Act 1983*, Australian government agencies must transfer records sentenced Retain as National Archives (RNA) either as soon as practicable after business use has ceased or at the latest 15 years after creation. However, the size and complexity of large-big datasets pose a challenge for transfer.
3. *Distributed custody:* section 64 of the *Archives Act* allows for permanent value records to remain in the custody of the controlling agency subject to certain conditions; however, not a single section 64 agreement has been developed for digital records.

Ultimately, the aim of the project was to inform NAA decision making and shape our guidance, especially around distributed custody arrangements for digital records.

Project method

The project was carried out by the Digital Archives Innovation and Research (DAIR) section of National Archives, in partnership with Governance Records Assurance, the section responsible for government recordkeeping. DAIR operates as something of a research hub for the National Archives and undertakes short-term projects of a few days (e.g. rapid evidence reviews) to longer-term projects typically up to 6 months.

The approach adopted for the Big Data Project was to interview national and international archives[9] and selected Australian government agencies[10] to gather information about their responses to these business problems. One-hour interviews were scheduled, and separate questions were developed for archival authorities and agencies. Each interview was recorded and detailed notes were written up, with overall results collated in spreadsheets.[11]

The following sections provide a brief overview of the results with a focus on a few key themes:

Government agencies

Size, range, and nature of datasets

The agencies interviewed can be broadly divided between those creating and managing research and scientific datasets, such as BOM and Geoscience Australia, and those managing datasets containing the personal information of Australian citizens and which relate to rights and entitlements, such as the Department of Social Services, the Australian Taxation Office (ATO), and Services Australia. Some agencies straddle both categories, for example, ABS and the Department of Agriculture, Fisheries and Forestry.

The agencies can be further categorized by those managing extremely large datasets in the petabyte size such as BOM and those like ABS managing hundreds or sometimes thousands of individual datasets that together amount to a very large quantity of data.

Records authorities

All of the interviewed agencies had retention and disposal schedules/authorities, referred to as RAs, though they varied widely in currency. Some agencies had detailed DIRKS-era[12] RAs, while others had streamlined 'rolled-up' RAs characterized by a smaller number of 'bucket' classes. A common theme from the interviews was that RAs were difficult to interpret and apply to data and datasets, partly because current records and information managers were not involved in their development. Most said that their RAs required updating either because they were too old and used outdated terminology or because they had significant gaps in coverage. A few felt that their RAs adequately covered their historical datasets but did not cover some current datasets. A number of agencies were already working on updating their RAs; however, it was a slow process because of limited resources and the need for wide stakeholder engagement.

Public access

Generally, the agencies creating and managing research and scientific datasets are already providing public access to their data, for example, from their websites like BOM and the ABS, from third-party providers like some Geoscience datasets, or from public data archives. These research datasets tend to be heavily used by the public.

The agencies creating and managing the private data of Australian citizens do not provide public access to this information though they may provide access to summary data for social research purposes. They are required to release private data to individuals as a result of freedom of information requests.

Distributed custody arrangements
All of the interviewed agencies expressed the need for distributed custody arrangements because of the size and complexity of their datasets and ongoing business needs that required retention of custody. Some agencies felt that distributed custody arrangements were appropriate due to the complexities involved in appraisal and disposal (including transfer) of massive datasets containing sensitive personal information (although it was understood that sensitivity does not exempt an agency from transferring records to the National Archives).

However, though accepting the need for distributed custody, all agencies expressed concerns about requirements that may be imposed under such agreements, in particular:

- The potential for significant additional costs, for example, the requirement for multiple redundant storage options
- Physical inspections, which some agencies said would not be possible for security reasons, and which in any case are not appropriate for digital records
- Access requirements under the Archives Act, especially for personal sensitive information
- Difficulties determining a custodian for shared data, i.e. data that is shared between multiple agencies or shared with in joint venture arrangements
- Any legal requirements such as insurance would need to be approved by legal teams and senior management.

On the other hand, some of the agencies said that many of the requirements for long-term preservation and access are already in place as part of normal data management and data protection practice.

Government archival authorities

Interviews were conducted with other national archives and a number of local archival jurisdictions both national and international (e.g. the Landesarchiv Baden-Württemberg).

Regulatory environment
The level and degree of information management regulation and compliance can be broadly split between countries whose legal systems are based on common law or civil (codified) law. In civil law countries, which include much of mainland Europe, many of the archival authorities' issue regulations or orders that have a relatively high level of agency compliance. The archival authorities often issue or endorse detailed functional requirements for business systems managing records and issue regulations requiring compliance with technical standards, including technical requirements for transfer.[13] Common law countries, such as United Kingdom, the United States, Canada, Australia, and New Zealand, may issue standards and guidance but tend not to enforce them, and agency compliance varies widely. In effect, in these countries, agencies self-regulate and there is a high degree of latitude in interpreting and applying guidance and standards.

In European countries, government agencies managing large-big datasets tend to be more aware of their records and information management responsibilities regarding data. This is partly because of stricter regulatory regimes, which mandate technical requirements for systems and transfer but also because they have considerable experience over many years in database preservation and transfer. Most of the key database preservation research projects have been European, such as the development of the Software Independent Archiving of Relational Databases (SIARD) format at the Swiss Federal Archives and the work of the European Union-funded E-Ark Project. Nevertheless, the interviews did indicate that even in Europe it can be difficult to find fully compliant agency business systems. One European archival authority said that they treat transfers as a snapshot of data at a point in time. They cannot guarantee the accuracy of the data as they cannot be responsible for agency information management practices, for example, if archival value data was overwritten as part of a thinning process.

Retention and disposal schedules
Most of the archival authorities said that retention and disposal schedules were required by law and should cover all information, including databases and datasets. Functions-based disposal schedules are commonly used, but most archival authorities said that disposal schedules generally did not adequately cover data and datasets. Most archival authorities reported large disparities in coverage between disposal schedules, for example, some take a 'big bucket' approach, while others are more granular. Often a permanent value business system or dataset was a single line in a disposal schedule although it may contain temporary or nonarchival information.

There was also broad agreement among archival authorities that retention and disposal schedules invariably do not help to determine the archival 'record' to be transferred from a database or business system to the archival authority. The Estonian National Archives adopted a macro-appraisal approach to determine the value of databases across government. For each archival value system, they conduct a high-level appraisal of the data within the business system, e.g. system files and views can be discarded. Other European archives have well-established transfer regimes and, as mandated in regulation, determine what is to be transferred when the business system is being developed. A common problem identified in the interviews is that records and information officers tend to take a narrow view of the record and often do not consider data and datasets as records.

Distributed custody arrangements
Under distributed custody arrangements a body other than the archival authority retains custody of archival value records, while control and ultimate responsibility for the records rests with the archival authority. While distributed custody arrangements are common for analogue records,[14] few if any have been established for digital records. The broad view across the interviewed archival authorities was that distributed custody arrangements for large-big datasets were desirable and that a practical and implementable management regime overseen by the archival authority was a necessary component of it.

Reflection
Two key findings of the project are that, for common law countries like Australia, (1) agencies are retaining custody of archival-value digital records that are eligible for transfer to the archival authority and (2) archives do not have distributed custody arrangements in place for those records.

The first point is well known. For archival authorities, the so-called digital deluge has been just around the corner for a couple of decades now, but so far the flood still hasn't eventuated. At the NAA, the vast bulk of the digital records received from agencies are from temporary agencies such as Royal Commissions or Commissions of Inquiry, closed agencies, or records for which there is no inheriting agency as a result of machinery of government change. If we expected regular transfers from standards-based systems like Electronic Document and Records Management Systems to become the norm, we were mistaken. In 2023, we should be receiving archival value records created in 2008 or earlier, but presumably they are still in the custody of agencies being managed in a recordkeeping environment that can only be described as post-custodial by default. The reasons for the lack of transfers are doubtless multifaceted and complex, and a recent Australasian Digital Records Initiative (ADRI) project investigated barriers to digital transfers in government jurisdictions in Australia and New Zealand. The report setting out the findings of the project will be published in late 2024.

The second point also requires explanation. As we've seen, the need for distributed custody arrangements for digital records was recognized as early as the mid-1990s, and the National Archives of Canada developed and published model terms and conditions for distributed custody arrangements. But even in Canada, it appears distributed custody arrangements for digital records have not been pursued.

One reason for the absence of distributed custody agreements for digital records was the development of digital preservation systems in the 2000s. Post-custodialism and distributed custody became influential in the 1990s because archival authorities did not have the infrastructure and systems to manage and preserve digital records. However, by the early 2000s, digital preservation standards and workflows began to be published and soon afterward, software solutions that implemented them became available. The National Archives abandoned distributed custody in 2000 when it embarked on a project, called Agency to Researcher, tasked with developing an in-house digital preservation program.[15] Public Record Office Victoria's (PROV) Victorian Electronic Records Strategy (VERS) appeared in 1996 and was the basis of its digital archive and digital preservation standards. A partnership between the UK National Archives and software company Tessella produced Safety Deposit Box in 2003, which was to become Preservica. By the second decade of the 2000s, there were many commercial and open-source digital preservation systems to choose from. There was nothing preventing archival authorities taking custody of digital records – all they had to do was wait for the records to arrive.

Another reason for the absence of distributed custody agreements is their complexity. They are legal instruments and therefore enforceable with penalties for noncompliance (typically, immediate transfer to the archive). The legal nature of the agreements means that finalizing them can be time-consuming process involving legal teams scrutinizing every provision. Agencies may be encouraged to enter distributed custody agreements if a more streamlined model was adopted, for example, a generic set of provisions and requirements that an agency could opt into. The proposed streamlined approach should not impose significant legal barriers for agencies, and as much as possible, the conditions should not impose any significant extra costs on the agency.

A third reason is due to the continuing lack of clear rules for care of the records for which distributed custody arrangements are required. For analog records, these special rules usually refer to storage and conservation standards. For digital records, well-known digital preservation maturity models such as the National Digital Stewardship Alliance (NDSA) Levels of Digital Preservation[16] and the DPC Rapid Assessment Model (RAM)[17] could be repurposed as a set of conditions within a distributed custody agreement.

Conclusion

In a 2017 article, Mpho Ngoepe argues that the South African National Archives (SANA) is unconsciously following a post-custodial approach to the preservation of digital records because SANA does not have the infrastructure to support the transfer, management, and preservation of digital records.[18] Consequently, at the time of publication, almost no agencies had transferred records to the archive. Records remained in the custody of the agency, but the concern, naturally, was that records were being lost.

Although, in contrast, almost all the archives interviewed for the Big Data Project did have the infrastructure and systems to accept transfers, most government archives are still not receiving them in a regular, scheduled way; you could say that, like South Africa, we're following a post-custodial approach by default.

This article argues that big data collections are prime candidates for distributed custody arrangements (as found in theoretical discussions dating back at least as far as the 1990s) as they are high value, have ongoing business use, and come with technical and financial barriers to their transfer into the custody of the archive. However, determining which components of these collections are for permanent retention as national archives and then establishing the special rules for big data collections are not necessarily easy undertakings. These special rules – the terms and conditions – are what we need to develop to ensure appropriate management and control of these distributed collections, without imposing unreasonable costs and unhelpful complexity.

Notes on contributor

Dr. James Doig has worked at the NAA for more than 20 years. In that time, he has worked in many roles in collection management, including digital preservation, transfer, description, and collection review. He has presented regularly at conferences such as Australian Society of Archivists (ASA) and Records and Information Management Practitioners Alliance (RIMPA) and has published articles in *Archives & Manuscripts*, *American Archivist*, and *Script & Print*. He is on the Research and Practice subcommittee of the Digital Preservation Coalition. He has a PhD in medieval history from Swansea University.

Acknowledgements

I would like to thank Rowena Loo for her comments on a draft of this article.

Notes

1. For this and what follows see Simon Davis, Looking Back to the Future: 30 Years of Keeping Electronic Records in the National Archives of Australia, National Archives of Australia, Canberra, 2004.
2. The e-permanence logo was a lower case 'e' engraved into a stone tablet, mimicking a cuneiform clay tablet. The blurb read: 'The e-permanence symbol represents the new standard in recordkeeping developed by the National Archives for use by all Commonwealth Government agencies. Though it applies to all forms of records, the new recordkeeping standard is particularly suited to deal with the challenges presented by the new electronic environment which has engendered an elusive and transitory quality to the Government's information assets'.
3. A revised version, *DIRKS: A Strategic Approach to Managing Business Information*, was released in 2001.
4. Heavily influenced by the work of David Bearman, see in particular Margaret Hedstrom and David Bearman, 'Reinventing Archives for Electronic Records: Alternative Service Delivery Options', in Margaret Hedstrom (ed.), Electronic Records Management Program Strategies, Archives and Museum Informatics, Pittsburgh, 1993, pp. 82–98. Cf. Adrian Cunningham's criticisms in 'Some Functions Are More Equal than Others: The Development of a Macroappraisal Strategy for the National Archives of Australia', Archival Science, vol. 5, 2005, pp. 163–84.
5. Terry Cook, 'Electronic Records, Paper Minds: The Revolution in Information Management and Archives in the Post-Custodial and Post-Modernist Era', Archives and Manuscripts, vol. 22, 1994, pp. 300–28. For the arguments of custodialists and post-custodialists during this period see Don Boadle, 'Reinventing the Archive in a Virtual Environment: Australians and the Non-Custodial Management of Electronic Records', Australian Academic & Research Libraries, vol. 35, no. 3, 2004, pp. 242–52, and Alistair G. Tough, 'The Post-Custodial/Pro-Custodial Argument from a Records Management Perspective', Journal of the Society of Archivists, vol. 25, no. 1, 2004, pp. 19–26.

6. Stephen Ellis and Steve Stuckey, 'Australian Archives' Approach to Preserving Long-Term Access to the Commonwealth's Electronic Records', in Stephen Yorke (ed.), Playing for Keeps: The Proceedings of an Electronic Records Management Conference, Hosted by the Australian Archives, Canberra, 8–10 November 1994, Australian Archives, Canberra, 1995, p. 128, https://web.archive.org/web/20050308142922/http:/ourhistory.naa.gov.au/library/playing_for_keeps.html.
7. Terry Cook, 'Leaving Archival Electronic Records in Institutions: Policy and Monitoring Arrangements at the National Archives of Canada', Archives and Museum Informatics, vol. 9, no. 2, 1995, pp. 141–9.
8. Ibid., p. 149.
9. National jurisdictions: US National Archives and Records Administration (NARA); National Archives of Finland; Archives New Zealand; Public Records Office, Northern Ireland; National Archives of Estonia; Danish National Archives; Swedish National Archives (Riksarkivet); UK National Archives (TNA). Local jurisdictions: Landesarchiv Baden-Württemberg; Public Records Office Victoria (PROV); State Records NSW; Queensland State Archives.
10. Australian Bureau of Meteorology (BOM); Australian Bureau of Statistics (ABS); Geoscience Australia; Commonwealth Scientific and Industrial Research Organisation (CSIRO); Department of Social Services; Department of Agriculture, Fisheries and Forestry; Australian Taxation Office (ATO); Services Australia.
11. Each recording was deleted after the interview was written up.
12. The DIRKS Manual was used in the Commonwealth government from 2000 to 2007.
13. For example, Norway has NOARK 5: https://www.arkivverket.no/forvaltning-og-utvikling/noark-standarden/noark5-standarden. The European DLM Forum has published modular requirements for records systems, MoReq2010.
14. CAARA Policy 15: https://www.caara.org.au/index.php/policy-statements/models-for-the-distributed-custody-and-management-of-government-archival-records/.
15. In 2000, the NAA released *Custody Policy for Commonwealth Records*, which signalled an in-principle undertaking to accept custody of all digital records appraised as having archival value, regardless of format. On the Agency to Researcher project see David Pearson and James Doig, 'Tales from "The disK Files": Lessons Learnt from a Data Recovery Project in 2003–2006 at the National Archives of Australia', The American Archivist, vol. 85, no. 2, 2022, pp. 361–2.
16. https://ndsa.org/publications/levels-of-digital-preservation/.
17. https://www.dpconline.org/digipres/dpc-ram.
18. Mpho Ngoepe, 'Archival Orthodoxy of Post-Custodial Realities for Digital Records in South Africa', Archives and Manuscripts, vol. 45, no. 1, 2017, p. 34, doi: 10.1080/01576895.2016.1277361.

REFLECTION

Paper Elephants: Reflections on Changing Archival Practice at the Australian Museum

Vanessa Finney[1,2]*

[1]World Cultures, Archives and Library, Sydney, Australia; [2]Australian Museum, Sydney, Australia

Abstract

The archives of Australia's first museum, the Australian Museum (AM) in Sydney, are an artefact of colonialism, still intertwined with the complexities of science, public museums, and imperialism. It's the elephant in the archival room. However, change has come to Australia's colonial-era museums, affecting their missions, historical framing, and collections and archives. This article provides a brief history of knowledge at the AM in order to showcase some current initiatives aimed at opening its archival holdings to new perspectives, encounters, shared knowledge, and a protocols-based approach to access. Understanding the history of the museum and its archival structures and methods is vital for rethinking a more open, generous, and responsible future for this important collection.

Keywords: *Museums*; *Museum archives*; *History of collections*; *Colonialism*; *Record-keeping*

The power and problem of the colonial archives

Empire, record-keeping, and archives are intimately linked. As archival theorists and historians of empire-building and colonisation have repeatedly shown, archival forms and record-keeping practices reflect and inform systems of governance, just as record-keeping was central to attempts by imperial powers and their colonies to assert and maintain administrative control.[1] It's an expanding critical arena, bringing together colonial historical studies and archival theory with studies that subject the colonial archives to sustained historical analysis. These studies view the archives themselves as 'artefacts of colonialism rather than simply the repositories where the data pertaining to the colonial past is stored'.[2] This thinking is also beginning to be reflected in changes to contemporary archival practice within some of Australia's most significant remaining colonial-era archival repositories.

Australia's first and oldest cultural-scientific institution, the Australian Museum (AM) in Sydney, was founded in 1827.[3] Its colonial archive documents the museum's own becoming and its developing knowledge practice in surprising detail. Still in use at the museum, it is one of only a few Australian colonial archives that continue to function in their original administrative context into the present.[4] This makes it a historical object in its own right and a place

*Correspondence: Vanessa Finney, Email: vanessa.finney@australian.museum

to reframe current practice. Following the lead of historians and theorists of the archive like Ann Laura Stoler, it is possible to use the AM Archives to both demonstrate and rethink the establishment and longitudinal operation of colonial archival power.

If, as museum theorist Tony Bennett suggests, museums are 'good to think with', then an archive within a natural history museum is even better.[5] We might be able to imagine a museum without objects, but it's impossible to think of a natural history museum without its archives to create and hold the conditions for its agency, knowledge, collections, and operations. At the AM, the museum's administrative recordkeeping rules and growing archival repository created and sustained the conditions of its authority and actions. At the same time, its specimen registration systems created and authorised its material forms and structured its scientific knowledge to circulate across worldwide networks of science and sociability. In part, this unique record-keeping system and the detailed paper trail it produced were a generative site for the universalist project to classify and order Australian nature and for the assertion of European ways of knowing across Australian landscapes and environments.[6]

As a clear mark of their continuing importance to the contemporary museum, the museum's colonial archives and their successors are still held largely in their original order on the same site in Sydney where they were created, ordered and used. Never transferred to the NSW State Archives, these institutional records remain within the neo-classical facade and sandstone walls of the museum. Never finished, the administrative and collection archives are still being added to and used. The archives now include a collected archive and a photography and moving image collection as well as a large digital archive.[7] The archival collections are vital to museum functioning and they are regularly accessed by museum staff and curators, scientists, historians, Indigenous communities, researchers and knowledge holders, and members of the public.

Legacies and potential

The AM spent its early decades establishing its own authority, and in protracted, and sometimes heated, private and public debate over its mission and leadership. Trust members, drawn from the colony's social and political establishment, were keen to generate and then share the spoils of the museum's specimen collections alongside its growing cultural and scientific networks, influence, and power. To read the early Trust Minutes is to see just how much time and energy was spent on rule-making and boundary riding.[8] Debates spilled into Parliament and the Sydney press too, where there was an avid public interest in the museum's governance and activities. Behind these debates were not just personal-political tussles, but some of the colony's most important, foundational tensions between nature, environment, and settlers, and between Indigenous presence and colonisers and settlers' aggressive claims for knowledge, territory, and authority.

In order to imagine the future, functions, and limits of the contemporary AM archive, it is vital to understand its staggered, uncertain history of becoming and the other possibilities for nature and museum practice its late 19th-century accounting and registration systems carefully papered over. There is a surprising fluidity to the museum's form and functions over these years. Creating a museum for the colony was an early state priority, but the animal taxonomies and collections focus that have come to define the public natural history museum were not the immediate priority. Rather they solidified as museum 'common sense' later in the century as the colony moved to nationhood, biological sciences moved to the university, taxonomic research moved behind the scenes and exhibitions and education became the museum's public face.[9] Before that, everything was up for messy, acrimonious debate – mission, governance, audience, material collections and built forms, scientific frameworks, and networks of influence. As part of this debate on its mission and values, the museum's recordkeeping systems – and especially who had the authority to make, keep, and authorise records – were argued over through the 19th century. This debate sometimes had dramatic results. The physical expulsion of curator Gerard Krefft from the museum building, along with his experimental scientific practice and his heretical evolutionary ideas, is the most graphic example.[10]

Of course, the past is never past. In some cases, the AM still uses the same colonial knowledge structures and some of its early recordkeeping series for making and keeping records today.[11] These records remain essential for taxonomic work, collection management and description, and historical research. However, understanding the museum's recordkeeping rules and archival materials, as well as their historical significance, allows them to become a central site for new museum taxonomies and other ontologies of nature. These same colonial archives, born in contestation and the quest for colonial power, are now of key significance in addressing a tangle of urgent epistemological and practical questions related to Indigenous data sovereignty, collection stewardship and repatriation, nature and 'country', biodiversity loss, climate change, and environmental sustainability. It's the task of those who work with these archives every day (archivists, but also data analysts, digitisation and preservation specialists, content producers, and curators) to make sure they are understood, accessible, known, and useful to help address these issues and more.[12]

It's a heady mix for a museum archivist, a chance to work at the coalface of critical museum practice and archival theory in a place that holds a complex documentary archive but is also, in itself, an archival object with its own fascinating potential for theorisation, history-making and historical description. With an understanding of this contingent history, it becomes possible to re-imagine contemporary archival practice at the museum to retain the archive as (historical) object but encircle that understanding with alternate contexts and descriptive regimes. We can open new pathways into (and out of) its archival structures and knowledge holdings to help expand and amplify its use. Postcolonial critiques of the archives become part of a reparative project.[13] Part of this is the work that historian and cultural practitioner Jilda Andrews calls 'cultural diplomacy', with the potential to redistribute museums' knowledges and cultural capital more equitably and more widely.[14] The 2024 NSW State Archives First-Nations-led community access project calls this 'rematriation' or 'the process of weaving traditional and cultural knowledge back in harmony with the land'.[15] As focussed on protocols as it is on holdings, this work can bring ways of being together to regenerate the museum and its archive less as a repository for text and things and for object-based thinking, and more as a dynamic and practical interface to community, country, knowledge, and story.[16]

There's one enormous built-in advantage to doing this work at the museum. Archives within museums have a ready-made on site and online audience, and a special opportunity and ability to reach outside their own orders, collections, and walls. The AM has an audience of over 1,000,000 visitors a year, with many more visiting the museum's website and viewing its regional touring exhibitions, events, and public programs. For the Archives team, it is an opportunity to work with urgent archival challenges in an institution committed to public communication, debate and the difficult process of 'unsettling' museum operations, collections, knowledges and narratives.[17]

Museums offer multiple pathways to connect issues, knowledge, and people: collections and catalogues, digital initiatives, digitisation and online content, apps and games, exhibitions, public programs, tours and talks, school and tertiary education programs, and research projects and collaborations. So how has AM archival practice responded to the colonial museum-archival challenge and to the wider need for more ethical, equitable, and critical modes of archival practice?

The elephant at the museum: is the museum an archive?

Work on historicising the colonial museum, along with new international definitions of the museum as an active, relational process, are moving museum archives and collection documentation to the centre of museum history, practice, and thought.[18] The idea of the 'relational museum' has grown alongside mass digitisation and big data approaches to museum specimens and collections, so that there is also a clearer view of the museum as a data and knowledge infrastructure and fact-making enterprise, alongside its material and object forms.[19] Increasingly, museums are studied as particular, historically contingent knowledge structures, processes, protocols, and relationships as much as they are for their collections and collectors.

The natural history museum has its own, particular methods and framework of 'common sense' tied to its scientific research and taxonomic discovery and classification functions. In part, the natural history museum wants to function as a kind of scientific instrument, doing two difficult and different things: making certified knowledge about nature, and then making that knowledge move. Like an archive, the natural history museum's operations and systems are focussed not just on keeping, but on classification and structuration for continuing motion and for agile access, use, and re-use of its knowledges into the future.[20]

In 1922, revered archival theorist Hilary Jenkinson posed an archival question that also goes to the heart of museum methods and thinking:

> Supposing for example that a Viceroy sends home to the Secretary of State in England an elephant with a suitable covering-note or label; ... the question may be imagined to arise: ... Is the elephant attached to the label or the label to the elephant?[21]

The obvious answer is that the label and the elephant need each other. Historical geographies, networks, and contexts matter, and it's relationships that count: between people, words, and things. Applying archival thinking to the museum allows us to look at its thing-making and world-making efforts across time and with an archival light. We can move on from the historical museum being the material baseline for discussions and interpretation to allow nuance and change in continuing museum practice.[22]

Re-making archival practice at the AM

What this shift means at the AM Archives is the recognition of the need for continual explication and promotion of its institutional archives as not just central but essential to museum history and to contemporary meaning-making at the museum. In practice, this has involved the small archives team working with collections and digitisation projects to embed archival thinking into digital initiatives, cataloguing protocols, data structures, and data linking projects. Using our museum advantage, a large part of our focus has been on public access and use. This has been expressed in new access regimes and protocols, in revised cataloguing protocols and priorities, as well as in exhibitions, research initiatives, and public histories.

In exhibitions and public programs showcasing the archives collections we have sought not just to showcase the fascinating and beautiful content of the AM archives, but at the same time to highlight their 'recordness', utility, and history. Colonial glass plate specimen photography collections, for example, were showcased in the *Capturing Nature* exhibition and book for their quirky beauty, as an undiscovered part of Australian photographic history, and as one of the earliest scientific uses of new photographic technologies in Sydney in the mid-19th century. They were also presented as part of the museum's innovative and experimental efforts to document its growing specimen collection and to reflect on developing museum-scientific practice.[23] *Transformations*, the book and exhibition based on the art and story of colonial natural history illustrators Harriet and Helena Scott featured their astounding natural art alongside a consideration of their life-long quest to be recorded and remembered in the archives of Australian science.[24]

External collaborations such as the cross-institutional and multi-disciplinary Australian Research Council project 'Merchants and Museums' focussed on 19th-century museum animal trade and exchange, have highlighted the power of archival records to recontextualise individual museum specimens within their historical narratives. Thinking archivally about museum animals and the paper trail that accompanies each animal as it moves through complex transaction events from field to museum and beyond has helped to understand museum meaning-making, reconstruct animal pathways, and recover the data deficit that can rob animal specimens and museum objects of their context, history, and future in museums.[25]

But re-making archival practice at the colonial museum requires more than research, exhibition, and the promotion of new archival stories. It means active, purpose-driven sharing and redistribution of archival power. The AM Archives most successful and long-term community-led 'cultural diplomacy' work has taken place around the Thomas Dick Birrpai Collection of photographs taken around Port Macquarie in the 1920s. The images document staged reconstructions of 'traditional' life and were taken by amateur photographer Thomas Dick working with local Birrpai families. The development of community-led access and research protocols for the collection over the past decade has been led by descendent and Birrpai elder Dr John Heath. This decades-long collaborative work with museum staff, community, and descendants of both the photographer and his subjects is a demonstration of the possibilities of generating and embedding a protocol-driven approach to archives. The collaboration has shown rethinking museum collections as community-led family histories can begin to redistribute museum knowledges and cultural capital.[26]

Perhaps the most important and long-lasting way to preserve the archival object we have while also pluralising its content and widening access pathways is to re-examine the AM archives' own historical and current protocols, knowledge structures, and descriptive standards. Understanding the history of previous museum recordkeeping and cataloguing practice is the first step, both their structures and order and their language and descriptive choices. With this understanding, we can provide more detailed context for reading and using the archives not only 'along the (colonial) archival grain', but as products of colonial knowledge structures and history. We can also begin to start reading them 'against the grain', looking for ambiguities, resistances, and processes of negotiation within the archive.[27]

Large-scale digitisation projects and new data tools can help us do this by making more visible the tight web of structuration and description that has made the archives so successful and useful as a knowledge tool. But digitisation is not just an opportunity to improve accessibility through the production and publishing of digital surrogates of archival documents. Just as importantly, accessibility can be enhanced and expanded through improving item-level descriptive metadata. With the help of dedicated volunteers, we are re-reading our colonial records (starting with correspondence, minutes and reports) for neglected and overlooked content and new layers within the existing record.[28] We are re-indexing these old records with new terms and emphases, applying new descriptive rules and adding new vocabularies and classifications. It's a semantic approach to redistributing and pluralising the archives' content that is surfacing new patterns, asking new questions, and revealing new relationships.

The enormous task of re-indexing the museum's Trust Minutes, for example, has unlocked this vital record for new levels of detail of collection documentation and institutional history. Beyond the 'who's who' approach of the creator of the initial Trust Minutes index, we have revealed layers of names, places, and webs of influence, unrecorded in previous indexes. With these new semantic pathways, spirals, and webs, new museum stories can be surfaced and told. Newly detailed indexes to the AM's pre-1900 outward correspondence series are allowing, for the first time, search and retrieval for hundreds of previously unrecorded names, places, and events, including new details of object custody, provenance, and history wrapped up and enclosed in letters on donations, trades, and exchanges. In her article 'Silence and resistance', writer Evelyn Araluen challenges us to consider the textual forms as well as the writing and representations of archival texts in order to 'resist, rewrite and reclaim' Aboriginal identities.[29] At the AM, the mundane and careful technical work of preparing these detailed indexes is helping to make both the contents of the archive and the process of archivalisation (more) visible. We are making the archive responsible.

The AM and its archive embody and enclose colonialist structures of knowledge, but they also hold the potential to help disrupt those structures and established ways of thinking and acting. This reframing can put the archives – with its elephants and its labels – at the centre of Museum history and future. We are only just getting started on thinking about new museum-archival practices and the possibilities (and challenges) for opening the archives to new ways of encountering, reading and using.

Notes on contributor

Dr Vanessa Finney is the Head of World Cultures, Archives, and Library at the Australian Museum. She has authored books and curated exhibitions on the role of photography in museums, including *Capturing Nature* (2018), and on colonial Sydney naturalists and artists Harriet and Helena Scott, titled *Transformations* (2017, 2024). Currently, she is writing a book on 19th-century practices of natural history at the Australian Museum in Sydney. Finney is a curator, archivist, and historian, holding a PhD in the History of Science from the University of Sydney.

Notes

1. Historian Bernard Cohn calls this 'epistemic colonialism'. Colonialism and Its Forms of Knowledge: The British in India (Princeton UP, New Jersey, 1996). For the work of archival repositories in colonialism's project, see Ann Laura Stoler, 'Colonial Archives and the Arts of Governance', Archival Science, vol. 2, 2002, pp. 87–109.
2. Tony Ballantyne, Webs of Empire: Locating New Zealand's Colonial Past, UBC Press, Vancouver, 2010, p. 189.
3. The AM opened its first public gallery in 1857 on William St opposite Hyde Park in the city's cultural heart.
4. Interestingly, several of these remaining in-situ colonial archives are held within other cultural and scientific institutions, bolstering the idea that there is a special connection between cultural/scientific institutions and archival authority and memory regimes. Other Sydney examples include SLNSW, AGNSW and Botanic Gardens.
5. Tony Bennett, 'Thinking (with) Museums: From Exhibitionary Complex to Governmental Assemblage', in K. Message and A. Witcomb (eds.), Handbook of Museum Studies, Wiley and Sons, Oxford, vol. 1, 2015, pp. 3–20.
6. My PhD investigates knowledge-practices at the nineteenth-century Australian Museum. Vanessa Finney, 'Putting Nature in Its Place: The Australian Museum, 1827–1890', PhD, University of Sydney, 2023.
7. For the holdings of the AM Archives see https://australian.museum/learn/collections/museum-archives-library/museum-archives/, accessed 10 February 2024.
8. Australian Museum Archives, AMS001, Trust Minutes, 1836.
9. In this move to orderly classification and a strict scientific rationale, the AM was following the general trend of nineteenth century natural history museums. See Susan Sheets-Pyenson, Cathedrals of Science. McGill UP, Montreal, 1988. The twin goals of collection and classification, and public education are still adhered to today. https://australian.museum/about/organisation/reports/, accessed 10 February 2024.
10. SMH, 'Krefft vs Hill', 19 November 1874.
11. Examples include Trust Minutes and collection registers (now incorporated into an electronic cataloguing system).
12. S. Das and M. Lowe were pioneers in highlighting this global work for natural history museums, 'Nature Read in Black and White: Decolonial Approaches to Interpreting Natural History Collections', Journal of Natural Science Collections, vol. 6, 2018, pp. 4–14.
13. Timothy Neale and Emma Kowal, '"Related" Histories: On Epistemic and Reparative Decolonization', History and Theory, vol. 59, no. 3, 2020, pp. 403–12.
14. Jilda Alice Andrews, 'Encountering Cultural Material in Museum Collections: An Indigenous Perspective', Phd, ANU, 2018.
15. https://mhnsw.au/news/improving-first-nations-community-access-to-archives/, accessed 23 April 2024.
16. This work will generate its own, new archive. Work on understanding the complex relationships and place of this future archive begins with critical thinking on data sovereignty. ATSIDA provides a model for this work. On cultural interface see Martin Nakata, 'The Cultural Interface', The Australian Journal of Indigenous Education vol 36, no 1, 2007, pp. 7–14.
17. 'Unsettled', an exhibition produced by the AM in 2002, was a path-making exhibition and community consultation project committed to First Nations led truth-telling about Australia's foundation stories.
18. The hotly contested process-based definition was approved by ICOM in 2022. https://icom.museum/en/resources/standards-guidelines/museum-definition/, accessed 10 February 2024.
19. On the relational museum see Mike Jones, Artefacts, Archives and Documentation in the Relational Museum, Routledge, London, 2021.
20. This is the great innovation of the Linnean system. It allows continual movement of individual animals within its base structuration of order, family, genus, species.
21. Hilary Jenkinson, A Manual of Archival Administration, Clarendon Press, Oxford, 1922.
22. Nicolas Thomas, 'The Museum as Method', Museum Anthropology, vol. 33, no. 1, 2010, pp. 6–10.
23. Vanessa Finney, Capturing Nature: Early Scientific Photography at the Australian Museum, NewSouth Publishing, Sydney, 2019.
24. Vanessa Finney, Transformations: Harriet and Helena Scott, Sydney's Finest Natural History Painters, NewSouth Publishing, Sydney, 2018.
25. For a case-study of the Australian lungfish see Vanessa Finney, 'Dining on Geologic Fish: Claiming the Australian Ceratodus for science', Journal for the History of Knowledge, vol. 3, no. 1, 2022, 1–14.
26. John Heath and Ashley Barnwell, 'From the Inside: Indigenous-Settler Reflections on the family Uses of the Thomas Dick "Birrpai" Photographic Collection 1910–1920', Life Writing, vol. 20, no. 1, 2023, pp. 163–82. The collection was a successful joint nomination for UNESCO Australian Memory of the World Register in 2023.

27. This is the critical methodology of Ann Laura Stoler in Along the Archival Grain: Epistemic Anxieties and Colonial Common Sense, Princeton UP, 2010.
28. This work could not have been done without the leadership and insight of archivist Robert Dooley and the transcription and indexing work of volunteers Cynthia Rodrigo, Prue Walker and Kerry Gordon.
29. Evelyn Araluen, 'Silence and Resistance: Aboriginal Women Working within and against the Archive', *Continuum*, vol. 2, no. 4, 2018, pp. 487–502.

REFLECTION

Research, Access, and Digitisation: Reflections on Responsible Stewardship in the Online Era

Jessica Moran*

Alexander Turnbull Library, Te Puna Mātauranga o Aotearoa National Library of New Zealand, Wellington, New Zealand

Abstract

This article reflects on the impact of digitisation programs for researcher access to archival materials. Using the author's experience as both a researcher using digitised material and as a manager of archival programs, the article considers the opportunities and challenges of researcher demand for digital access and suggests the archival value of responsible stewardship is a useful concept when navigating access in the online era.

Keywords: *Digitisation; Archival values; Research use; Responsible stewardship; Access.*

Most of my career in archives has been as a practitioner undertaking practice-based research, assessment, and analysis. Archival theory has informed and guided my work and how I think about that work, but so has my experience as a researcher on the other side of the desk. This has particularly affected how I think about access and use of archives. While preservation is a key component of digitisation programs and projects I've been a part of, access is the ultimate goal. Digitisation can extend the reach of archival materials, make archival material more visible, unlock material that can't easily be consulted or used without intervention, or allow users to access archives without coming into a physical archive and often without any direct contact with staff.

There is a growing body of research looking to understand and measure the use and impact of digitised archival and other primary source materials.[1] There is an equally growing awareness that digitisation – especially our efforts to make more of our collections available online – constitutes a kind of collection building with a profound effect on what material is used and the consequent research outputs from those collections.[2] Finally, digitising and making archives available online takes sustained effort and resources, with growing digital storage impacting our environment.

This has led me to consider three things: first, the kind of digital archives we're creating when we digitise holdings and the kind of research this enables; second, the kind of research we disadvantage; and, when considering the research and experience of the library and archival community over the past 15–20 years, the degree to which our digitisation practice has (or

*Correspondence: Jessica Moran Email: jessica.moran@dia.govt.nz

should have) changed to support researchers. To do this, I'm going to draw upon my experience as a manager and steward of archival collections and digitisation projects, and my work as a researcher and editor, to reflect on use, collection building, access, and sustainability.

My reflections in this piece are influenced by my positionality. I self-identify as both a White American and Pākeha New Zealander; I am middle class and have more than one graduate degree. I have worked in libraries and archives for over 20 years, mostly in research libraries or archives in the United States and New Zealand. From early in my career, I have been motivated to make archival materials more accessible, easy to find and use, and have seen online access as a powerful tool toward this goal.

In 2016, I worked on an independent project to co-edit the book *Prison Memoirs of an Anarchist* by Alexander Berkman.[3] Originally published in 1912, the book provides an account of Berkman's attempt to assassinate Henry Clay Frick for his role in suppressing the strike at the Carnegie-owned Homestead Steelworks in 1892 and his subsequent 14 years in prison. It is considered a classic of prison literature[4] – a memoir of the author's psychological struggles and growth over 14 years in prison, as well as a documentary account of the anarchist and prison milieus surrounding him. The aim of our project was to provide an annotated edition that drew out the names, place, legal details, and contemporary literary and political references that might not otherwise be accessible to modern readers. As part of the project, we also transcribed and edited a previously unpublished diary Berkman kept while writing his memoirs.

At the time, my co-editor and I were living in New Zealand and travel to the various archives across the US and Europe that held the relevant records and papers was not feasible. Instead, we managed the project mostly with digitised sources, something that would not have been possible even 10 years earlier. Our main primary sources for this work were: the Alexander Berkman papers (including the diary) held and digitised by the International Institute for Social History in the Netherlands[5]; digitised photographs from the Library of Congress; and digitised newspapers from New York and the Pittsburgh, Pennsylvania area available through the commercial database Newspapers.com. We also sourced digitised copies of materials including out-of-print books, journals, and pamphlets available through independent online community archives of anarchist and socialist history. Using sources that spanned both national and institutional boundaries allowed us to identify and locate relevant and required material. We could only do this effectively because so much of the material we needed was digitised.

The availability of digitised material had a fundamental impact on my ability to undertake the research and to successfully create a new body of work based on archival sources. Digitising material, especially archival content that cannot otherwise be used without traveling around the globe, creates the possibility for new kinds of research projects. The standard of digitisation did not matter to me as long as I could read the content. For handwritten documents, it did help to be able to view the items on a larger screen where I could zoom in to decipher handwriting, but overall I just needed the quality of digitised material to be good enough to read on a screen and in a few cases reproduce for publication.

Use of digitised archives

How does this compare with research on researcher requirements?[6] As a profession, we've been asking this question since we started digitising in earnest. In 2013, Alexandra Chassanoff found that historians were using digitised sources (among others) in their research.[7] However, at that time many expressed concerns over the quality of the digital reproduction and the trustworthiness of the sites (preferring recognised libraries and archives over other online digitised material), while some argued that they would still rather access the items in person rather than online. Historians also reported that they wanted full runs of newspapers or entire collections digitised rather than individual items. A more recent study found a growing use of digitised archival material, but the lack of transparency about exactly what from a collection had been digitised and how led to feelings that ranged from a sense the archives were 'quietly incomplete' to the more violent 'virtual dismemberment'.[8] From my own experience, complete digitised collections – whether an entire archival collection, a manuscript, a newspaper, or a journal – were important, both when I was looking for a particular piece of information and when I wanted to be sure that I'd reviewed everything I could find on a topic. My professional background made it easy for me to quickly understand what kind of repository I was looking at. And I was less concerned with both trustworthiness and quality of reproduction than I was with my ability to access the material, though this may be because I trusted my own abilities to judge the authenticity of sources.

Recent evidence suggests a preference for using digitised archives. A 2021 survey in the United States as part of the Building a National Finding Aid Network Project found that over 50% of respondents either preferred or only wanted to use online sources, and only 14.7% preferred in-person access to materials.[9] To put simply, these results show that the vast majority – almost 85% – would either prefer or be equally happy accessing archival material online, rather than coming into a reading room. Even if this accurately reflects how most people work (or want to work) with archives, I wonder if professionally we are continuing to privilege the physical reading room, just as Paul Macpherson argued in 2010, because of the value we place on the sort of long and deep engagement with archival material that can happen there.[10] As Macpherson notes, the arguments against privileging digital and online access are compelling, particularly for traditional stakeholders. Not everything is (or can be) digitised, so historians and other researchers need access to physical material too. Relying on digitisation for access could prevent the creation of new knowledge and research. The lack of universal internet access means over-emphasis on digital use could impact the most economically and culturally marginalised people in society. And some people will always need access to the originals. These are all valid arguments that need to be carefully consider before shifting resources from staffing in-person reading rooms to making more materials available online.

And yet, we know we can increase the reach and impact of archives with online access. For example, those most economically and culturally marginalised may also be least likely to afford the time and money required to visit the reading room in person. It seems what our organisations have attempted to do is split the difference and try to prioritise both. We keep our reading rooms staffed at the same levels we always have in order to serve our in-person users while also increasing digitisation efforts and making more materials available online. The challenge becomes sustainability as we try and do more to serve our users without additional resources or changes in our practices.

Archival values & what to digitise
As a profession, our values include access to and use of records, preservation of records and archives, and support for the important role they play in memory, history, and accountability.[11] As a practitioner, these values can feel they are in opposition, but the important work is in balancing them in the service of improved access and use. It is through the use of archives, records, and other documentary heritage that we understand and make sense of our history and are accountable to history, memory, and truth(s). It is also through use that archives remain not only preserved but meaningful into the future. We must find new ways to grow and support digitisation efforts as one way of improving access to the collections, even as we know that only a sliver of the vast archives held will be digitised anytime soon.[12] When I think about myself as a researcher, or my experience working with other researchers, I have found

people want to be able to find and access the records they're looking for in the easiest or most frictionless way. That doesn't mean that all material should be delivered and accessible to all uniformly. It means that everything, from how we describe archives in online finding aids and catalogs to conditions of access and use, should be made clear and easy to understand.

Figuring out what to digitise becomes a critical challenge when I consider archival values and researcher access. Knowing that we've collected archives for accountability, memory, and history, knowing that while few may use them, they have lasting impact, and knowing that our users want to access material remotely, online, at a distance and are likely never to visit the reading room, how do we decide what to digitise?

Two strands guide my thinking when it comes to determining selection. The first is that digitisation programs are a form of appraisal and collection development. What we make available online becomes an 'archive' and is for many (most?) of our users, their only understanding of what an institution holds. Our decisions about what we digitise and make available must be made with as much rigor and integrity as we do when we make appraisal decisions about what comes into an archive.[13] Here I continue to be influenced by Terry Cook's thinking that archives should 'reflect multiple voices, and not by default only the voices of the powerful, an archival legacy shaped by an appraisal respecting diversity, ambiguity, tolerance, and multiple ways of archival remembering, celebrating difference rather than monoliths, multiple rather than mainstream narratives'.[14]

To do this through digitisation is a chance to rethink our holdings and the stories they can tell online. But I am also guided by my experience as a researcher who wants to read through the *whole* archive, who wants to know all the context, and who hopes to find lost gems hidden in a folder no one (except the processing archivist) has looked at before. This is one reason mass newspaper digitisation is so popular with researchers, from professional historians to genealogists – the obvious pleasure of being able to search across a whole corpus to find the particular bit of information you've been searching for. But this is only possible for newspapers because these particular records have 'made the cut'. Until recently, digitisation selection has been driven by a few key imperatives. The material had to be out of copyright or cleared copyright with rights holders, well described, physically easy to digitise, and visually appealing or already identified as a high value/high use collection. None of these criteria necessarily had to do with building more inclusive collections. They were by necessity concerned with what was possible and justifiable, within the legal and technical parameters that governed the institutions.

As our digitisation programs have matured, I see the future of our work being focused in two areas. The first is on-demand one-off digitisation required by researchers of material not yet digitised to fulfil individual researcher needs in the moment. The second, and where we should focus our energy, is the digitisation of whole collections so that researchers have the option to view what is in every folder, every line of a diary, or all of the meeting minutes and reports.[15] As an added benefit, this type of digitisation is likely to be of more use for computational research. This is not to say that issues of rights clearance, cultural responsibilities to Indigenous sovereignty over archival records, and our ethical responsibilities to the lives of those represented in archival records should be second to the rights of researchers to access material but rather to acknowledge that when appropriate, what is most useful to most users is access to entire collections or archives in context, rather than individual documents in isolation.[16]

Sustainability and responsible stewardship

As archivists, we aim to expand the reach of archives and connect them locally and across the globe, so that those for whom the information is important can grasp it and use it. I want this to be done ethically and responsibly. This work is an opportunity for our institutions to be in service to the values of accountability, memory, remembering, and history. But these values push up against our equally important role to be responsible stewards. As responsible stewards, we need to sustainably manage our institutions and to be responsive to the pressures that our digital work can put on our already strained infrastructure. Is it sustainable and ethical to continue to collect, to operate in-person reading rooms, controlled climate storage repositories, and exponentially growing digital collections of born-digital and digitised content knowing both the increasingly large impact they have on our climate, and the small and strained budgets under which archival institutions operate?[17]

The awareness that responsible stewardship must be a key value underpinning decision-making in archival organizations can help us navigate through this moment.[18] Our work is in some sense all about managing polarities: the need to support deep research in reading rooms with the need for access across geographical boundaries to archival records; the need to protect the rights of creators, copyright holders, traditional owners of information held in archives, and the personal privacy of those documented, with the need to provide access in support of memory, accountability, and truth telling; the need to be responsive to our researchers by providing the best access we can, with the economic and environmental pressure of more and more digital storage and infrastructure.[19] Shifting our thinking from ownership and custody of archives to stewardship by necessity involves inviting more people into the project of preservation and access to archival records. And it gives us room to be honest about the difficult decisions we make every day. It helps in deciding how to prioritise and fund access to archival records, in determining what to digitise, and to what sort of standards. It can help us understand how our 'best practices' can facilitate decision-making while also getting in the way of new and innovative ways to be of service to record creators, those with an interest in the records, and those who would like to use the records. This requires working in partnership with all interested stakeholders and communities to understand what we should digitise while continuing to research and evaluate our preservation and storage standards and their environmental impacts.

Becoming responsible stewards is to become comfortable with giving up some of the power that comes with ownership. Thinking about access as a binary open or closed isn't helpful. This might mean digitising material for a specific community to use without making it openly accessible online for all. We can consider 'good enough' digitisation at lower resolution and with smaller file sizes if it is serving user needs to access, read, and use the content. Within my own work, one example has been experimenting with a controlled digital access model based on trust.[20] We can find new ways to provide access to archival records from controlled digital access and virtual reading rooms to digital repatriation.

Thinking back to my example of using archival materials across institutional and national boundaries to complete a research project, it was not one archive or one collection that allowed for the project's success but rather the web of archives from those in traditional archival institutions, to commercial services, to community digital archives. Doesn't this in a small way, point toward the post-custodial future F. Gerald Ham envisioned?[21] Our own research in the archives and about the archives, and the research of archival users ultimately must affect the kinds of decisions, we make about digitisation and access. As Michelle Light has stated, 'in a postcustodial approach, archivists are experts, but not the only experts in archival decision-making'.[22] We are still some time away from a post-custodial archival environment but considering the challenges to the archival project we face from building more reflective and diverse collections, to the impact of our work on a changing climate, to supporting memory, truth, and accountability in an increasingly polarised political world, the concept and value of responsible stewardship helps us navigate into the future.

Notes on contributor

Jessica Moran (she/her) is the Acting Chief Librarian at the Alexander Turnbull Library, Te Puna Mātauranga o Aotearoa National Library of New Zealand. Her substantive role is Associate Chief Librarian, Research Collections where she is responsible for managing curatorial, digital collections, digitisation projects, and archival processing for the Library. In the 11 years she's been at the Alexander Turnbull Library, she has worked as a digital archivist and head of Digital Collections Services, before becoming Associate Chief Librarian in 2021. She has worked to help other libraries and archives get started with managing born digital collections and ensuring that our diverse digital cultural heritage is preserved. Prior to moving to New Zealand in 2012, she worked in university, special, and government libraries and archives in California, including the California State Archives. Jessica has a Masters in History from San Francisco State University and in Library and Information Science from San Jose State University.

Notes

1. See, for example, Ian Milligan, 'The Transformation of Historical Research in the Digital Age', in Cambridge Elements of Historical Theory and Practice, https://www.cambridge.org/core/elements/transformation-of-historical-research-in-the-digital-age/30DFBEAA3B753370946B7A98045CFEF4, accessed 5 August 2022.
2. See, for example, Kaspar Beelen, Jon Lawrence, Daniel C S Wilson and David Beavan, 'Bias and Representativeness in Digitized Newspaper Collections: Introducing the Environmental Scan', Digital Scholarship in the Humanities, vol. 38, no. 1, April 2023, pp. 1–22, doi: 10.1093/llc/fqac037 and Catherine Nicole Coleman, 'Managing Bias When Library Collections Become Data', International Journal of Librarianship, vol. 5, no. 1, 2020, pp. 8–19, doi: 10.23974/ijol.2020.vol5.1.162.
3. Alexander Berkman, Prison Memoirs of an Anarchist, Jessica Moran and Barry Pateman (eds.), AK Press, Chico, CA, 2017.
4. See, for example, John William Ward, 'Violence, Anarchy, and Alexander Berkman', The New York Review of Books, November 5, 1970.
5. Alexander Berkman Papers, International Institute for Social History, https://hdl.handle.net/10622/ARCH00040.
6. I've chosen to use the term researcher as a catch all for anyone who has an information need that can be found in the archives, rather than further segment the types of users who consult archives.
7. Alexandra Chassanoff, 'Historians and the Use of Primary Source Materials in the Digital Age', The American Archivist, vol. 26, no. 2, Fall/Winter 2013, pp. 458–80.
8. Donald Force and Bradley Wiles, '"Quietly Incomplete": Academic Historians, Digital Archival Collections, and Historical Research in the Web Era', Journal of Contemporary Archival Studies, vol. 8, 2021, https://elischolar.library.yale.edu/cgi/viewcontent.cgi?article=1140&context=jcas, accessed 17 November 2023.
9. Lesley A Langa, Chela Scott Weber and Lynn Silipigni, Pop-Up Survey: Findings from the Building a National Archival Finding Aid Network Project, OCLC, Dublin, OH, 2023, doi: 10.25333/qfjb-h531.
10. Paul Macpherson, 'Building a Better Horse and Buggy: The Privileging of Access in Reading Rooms Over Online Access', Archives & Manuscripts, vol. 38, no. 2, November 2010, pp. 61–78.
11. Australian Society of Archivists, Mission, Goals and Values, https://www.archivists.org.au/about-us/mission-goals-and-values, accessed 17 November 2023, Archives and Records Association of New Zealand Te Hunga Mahara, Code of Ethics, https://www.aranz.org.nz/code-of-ethics, accessed 17 November 2023, Society of American Archivists, SAA Core Values Statement and Code of Ethics, https://www2.archivists.org/statements/saa-core-values-statement-and-code-of-ethics, accessed 17 November 2023.
12. See Verne Harris, 'The Archival Sliver: Power, Memory, and Archives in South Africa', Archival Science, vol. 2, nos. 1–2, 2002, pp. 63–86.
13. Jessica Moran, Which Taonga First: Updating the Digitisation Selection Process at the Alexander Turnbull Library, OSF, October 2018, https://osf.io/ndvup/, accessed 17 November 2018.
14. Terry Cook, 'We Are What We Keep; We Keep What We Are: Archival Appraisal Past, Present and Future', Journal of the Society of Archivists, vol. 32, no. 15, December 2011, pp. 173–89.

15. This kind of digitisation requires significant investment, from research into selection for digitization, the detailed description required to digitize everything, to the infrastructure so people can easily search or read through an entire digitized collection. While I might want far more digitized, I know it doesn't come without a high price.
16. See, for example, Tara Robertson, 'Not All Information Wants to be Free: The Case Study of On Our Backs', in Applying Library Values to Emerging Technology: Decision-Making in the Age of Open Access, Maker Spaces, and the Ever-Changing Library (Publications in Librarianship #72), American Library Association, Chicago, IL, 2018, pp. 225–39, Rose Barrowcliffe, Lauren Booker, Sue McKemmish and Kirsten Thorpe, 'Activating and Supporting the Tandanya Adelaide Declaration on Indigenous Archives', Archives & Manuscripts, vol. 49, no. 3, 2021, pp. 167–85, doi: 10.1080/01576895.2021.1961086, Mark Crookston, Gillian Oliver, Ariana Tikao, Paul Diamond, Chern Li Liew and Sarsha-Leigh Douglas, 'Kōrero Kitea: Ngā hua o te whakamamatitang the Impacts of Digitised te reo Archival Collections', Report and Analysis of the Online Survey, 2016, InterparesTrust, http://interparestrust.org/assets/public/dissemination/Korerokiteareport_final.pdf, accessed 17 November 2023, Indigenous Archives Collective, 'Indigenous Archives Collective Position Statement on the Right of Reply to Indigenous Knowledge and Information Held in Archives', https://indigenousarchives.net/indigenous-archives-collective-position-statement-on-the-right-of-reply-to-indigenous-knowledges-and-information-held-in-archives/, accessed 17 November 2013, and Stephanie Carroll Rainie, Tahu Kukutai, Maggie Walter, Oscar Luis Figueroa-Rodríguez, Jennifer Walker and Per Axelsson, 'Issues in Open Data: Indigenous Data Sovereignty', in Tim Davies, Stephen B Walker, Mor Rubinstein and Fernando Perini (eds.), The State of Open Data: Histories and Horizons, African Minds and International Development Research Centre, Cape Town and Ottawa, 2019, pp. 300–19, http://stateofopendata.od4d.net, accessed 17 November 2023.
17. Jan Zastrow, 'The Environmental Impact of Digital Preservation – Can Digital Ever Go Green?', Computers in Libraries, vol. 42, no. 10, December 2022, https://www.infotoday.com/cilmag/dec22/Zastrow--The-Environmental-Impact-of-Digital-Preservation-Can-Digital-Ever-Go-Green.shtml, accessed 17 November 2023, Benjamin Matthew Goldman, 'It's Not Easy Being Green(e): Digital Preservation in the Age of Climate Change', in Christine Weideman and Mary A Caldera (eds.), Archival Values: Essays in Honor of Mark Greene, Society of American Archivists, Chicago, 2019, https://scholarsphere.psu.edu/resources/381e68bf-c199-4786-ae61-671aede4e041, accessed 17 November 2023, and Eira Tansey, A Green New Deal for Archives, Council on Library and Information Resources, Alexandria, VA, July 2023, https://www.clir.org/pubs/reports/a-green-new-deal-for-archives/, accessed 17 November 2023.
18. Michelle Light, 'From Responsible Custody to Responsible Stewardship', in Christine Weideman and Mary A Caldera (eds.), Archival Values: Essays in Honor of Mark A. Green, Society of American Archivists, Chicago, 2019, https://digitalscholarship.unlv.edu/lib_articles/590/, accessed 17 November 2023.
19. Jillian Cuellar, Audra Eagle Yun, Jennifer Meehan and Jessica Tai, 'Defining Archival Debt: Building New Futures for Archives', Journal of Contemporary Archival Studies, vol. 10, 2023, Article 8, https://elischolar.library.yale.edu/jcas/vol10/iss1/8, accessed 17 November 2023.
20. Sarah Walker, Valerie Love and Jessica Moran, 'The Virtus of Virtual: Piloting a Virtual Reading Room at the Alexander Turnbull Library, National Library of New Zealand', ASA Conference Paper, Brisbane, 16 September 2021 and Valerie Love, 'Can't Come to Wellington?: Exploring Controlled Digital Access for Digital Collections at the Alexander Turnbull Library', Turnbull Library Record, vol. 55, 2023, pp. 54–65.
21. F Gerald Ham, 'Archival Strategies for the Post-Custodial Era', American Archivist, vol. 44, no. 3, 1981, pp. 207–16.
22. Light, 'From Responsible Custody to Responsible Stewardship'.

REFLECTION

A Student's Reflection on the Digital Heritage Lab

Bryony Cavallaro*

Abstract

This is a reflection on my professional placement at Swinburne University's Digital Heritage Lab, exploring the role the lab plays in the preservation of Australian digital artefacts like computer software, video games and media artworks. As technology advances, the lab confronts the challenges posed by obsolete infrastructure, machine dependency, and the fleeting window of opportunity for preservation. The absence of standardised guidelines is addressed through collaborative efforts within the EaaSI (Emulation as a Service Infrastructure) network. My placement provided firsthand experience of the variety of challenges associated with digital preservation, emphasising the need for ongoing experimentation and perseverance in the face of failure. The experience gained from the placement underscores the importance of developing ideas and approaches through practical application in the field of digital archiving.

Keywords: *Digital archives*; *Digital preservation*; *University placement*; *AusEaaSI*; *Emulation as a Service Infrastructure*

With my Master of Information Studies (Charles Sturt University) concluding in 2023, it was time for me to make a pilgrimage to Melbourne for my professional placement. I had the privilege of visiting the Digital Heritage Lab at the Centre for Transformative Media Technologies at Swinburne University under the watchful care of Dr Cynde Moya. While there, I had a crash course in the practicalities of preserving digital artefacts, like computer software, video games, and media artworks. This piece discusses the work the Digital Heritage Lab is doing, and reflects on the relationship between my university coursework and practice in the lab and the value of experimentation and perseverance when tackling technical issues unique to digital preservation.

The Digital Heritage Lab is a paradise for anyone interested in vintage technology. Its shelves are lined end to end with plastic tubs labelled and categorised by type, containing all sorts of connectors, cables, and converters for a variety of hardware. There is a vast array of computers ranging from antiquated Commodore 64, Macintosh and Windows PCs, to older gaming consoles like the Nintendo Gameboy, along with a huge collection of older computer software, floppy disks, cartridges, cassettes, and CD-ROMs containing a variety of digital artefacts by Australian studios and artists (Figure 1). The beauty of the collection cannot be

---

*Correspondence: Bryony Cavallaro, Email: bryony.cavallaro@sl.nsw.gov.au

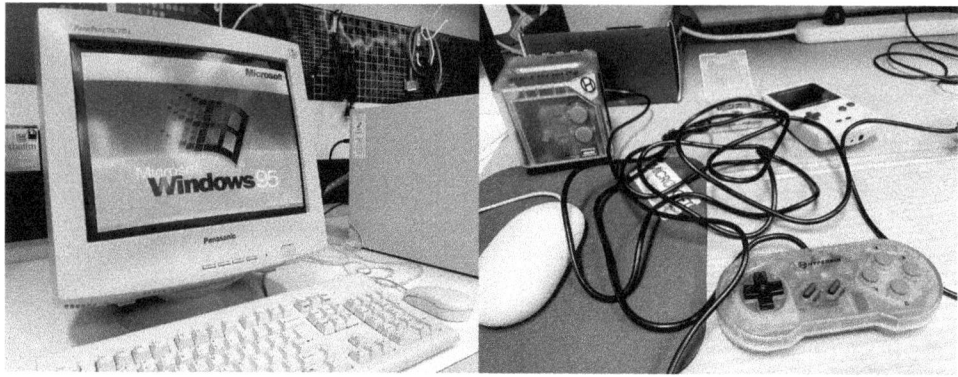

Figure 1. Desktop running Windows 95; and a Gameboy and other equipment in the Digital Heritage Lab. Photos: Bryony Cavallaro.

overstated, and Dr Moya keeps it well-stocked with anything obscure or rare (I was not aware that D15HD Male to Male converters for computers existed before my visit!).

The lab collaborates with memory institutions around Australia. It aims to: develop best practice methods for stabilising and preserving artwork and software; provide emulated access to artworks and software for research purposes; and investigate possibilities to re-display historic media artworks.[1] As technology continues to advance at breakneck speed, older pieces of software like interactive media artworks and vintage video games can quickly become inaccessible to both the public and researchers alike as the hardware required to run them becomes outdated, obsolete, or increasingly difficult to source. A CD-ROM with an artist's work could be scratched or damaged due to dust and poor storage conditions – for example, when kept in someone's home office since the mid-nineties – with the files only accessible on a Windows 95 operating system. Will that artwork therefore be lost, or is there something we as digital archivists can do to save it? The Digital Heritage Lab is in a unique position to offer solutions for researchers with its impressive hardware collection, and onsite staff with extensive knowledge.

The preservation of digital media heritage is a topic that continues to gain traction in Australia. Many libraries and museums are starting to take note of the importance of preserving significant digital artefacts like computer art installations from the nineties or video games developed on Australian soil, making the Digital Heritage Lab's mission, contents, and team particularly important. Many stakeholders, including the Art Gallery of NSW (AGNSW), the Australian Centre for the Moving Image (ACMI), and the State Library of NSW (SLNSW), rely on the assistance of the Digital Heritage Lab for its unique solutions, as well as for training in specific programmes like Applesauce and KryoFlux, both used for imaging floppy disks.

Preserving complex digital artefacts like video games and digital artworks demands knowledge across many different archiving specialities. Staff need to know about everything from collection management to audiovisual archiving. During my placement, the information I ended up applying the most was from the university course I did the previous year on Digital Curation and Preservation. But while I had completed plenty of practical assessments during my degree, covering a variety of library and records management skills – from cataloguing images to creating records management plans for fictional local councils – the practical tasks associated with digital archiving were less robust. I found myself wondering what else could be covered, such as tutorials on navigating antiquated GUIs, or the importance of checksum validation to monitor bit rot (the deterioration of digital data).

Being on the proverbial 'front line' also had unique challenges, the most obvious being the experimental nature of the work. When practice-based research is conducted on the outer edges of knowledge, there is little to no academic support available, nor is there unanimity on what constitutes 'best practice'. During my placement at the lab, I often found the specific knowledge I needed on internet forums like Reddit, or in YouTube videos from hobbyists. I also often spoke to Dr Moya about her preferences for things such as video quality or frame rate when I captured gameplay, as standards differ between institutions.

My university coursework also put a lot of emphasis on the risks associated with preserving digital data and the unique challenges digital objects present in comparison to their 'analogue' or paper counterparts. This is the idea that you can leave a piece of paper alone in a drawer for 50 years and still retrieve the contents, but the same cannot be said for a USB stick. Where the university took the time to discuss the multitude of problems associated with preserving digital artefacts, the lab spent less time on this and more on practical efforts to come up with solutions. Examples include emulation efforts through Emulation as a Service Infrastructure (EaaSI), disk imaging to capture fragile software, and recording gameplay of vintage games so that at least some semblance of the content is preserved for the future.

I understand that universities are there to provide a foundational understanding of the subjects one is studying, but I was surprised that the lab had such a 'keep trying until it sticks' approach. During my time at university, I read about several major risks unique to preserving digital data, as described by Howell,[2] and Oliver and Harvey,[3] such as:

(1) Physical degradation of the carriers of digital data;
(2) Difficulties accessing digital material due to the required software and hardware being obsolete or updated;
(3) The vulnerability of digital materials to unique perils such as malware infection and equipment failure;
(4) Insufficient resources to ensure preservation over a longer period of time;
(5) Loss of contextual information, making material unintelligible or inaccessible (including loss of password protection and encryption metadata);
(6) A lack of time or skills available to ensure the preservation of digital material;
(7) A lack of recognition of the digital material's value at the time of acquisition, resulting in deletion, loss, or change; and,
(8) A lack of standardised practice, leading to inconsistencies across organisations.

Thinking about the major risks that digital artefacts are vulnerable to, I witnessed some of these being actively addressed in practice at the Digital Heritage Lab.

The first risk relates to digital information's life expectancy based on the integrity of the carriers. This could be the physical degradation of CD-ROMS, floppy disks, or USB sticks, or the accessibility of older internet websites and links. All are susceptible to corruption and wear and tear, in part because these media were designed for obsolescence – the assumption that something newer and better would take their place. The lab circumvents this risk by imaging software to save digital backups that can be accessed via emulators in case of future degradation, as well as keeping the carriers themselves in a controlled environment. Another technique I witnessed was the keeping of multiple copies. If, for example, some data bits on a floppy disk become unreadable, a second copy of the disk may contain the information that was previously lost. Combining the two acts as a kind of 'restoration'.

The second risk I saw being a challenge was machine dependency. The lab is aware that eventually there will be no way to maintain older computers as parts that are no longer manufactured become increasingly sparse, and the implicit knowledge of experienced repairers is lost. Emulation is one way around the machine dependency concerns facing digital archivists today. The lab had been working with the EaaSI research programme, which acted as a browser-based computer emulator. Originally developed by Yale University Library, EaaSI was funded to link US libraries together, enabling the sharing of computer software across institutions.[4] The Australian Emulation Network, led by Professor Melanie Swalwell, focuses on collecting and providing access to high value collection items from the GLAM sector that require legacy computer environments to be accessed. AusEaaSI aims to have the same decentralised sharing network across Australia and New Zealand memory institutions. A virtual machine copy of past operating systems like Windows 95 or Mac 9.2.1 could be used within a modern browser system to load and access older software. The lab is in contact with 14 memory institutions in both Australia and New Zealand, creating a network of active participants interested in preserving the digital heritage of both countries.

The third challenge the lab is tackling is the short window of opportunity we currently have to preserve these complex digital artefacts. Dr Moya had previously worked for the Living Computer Museum in Seattle, Washington for a decade, and brought with her extensive experience working with vintage computer systems and their software. This knowledge is shared freely with other information professionals across Australia in need of specific advice regarding vintage hardware and software. Regularly communicating and assisting partner institutions allow the lab to emphasise the sense of urgency required to collect and preserve Australian media projects. The Digital Heritage Lab regularly hosts meetings with institutions like the State Library of South Australia, the Australian Computer Museum and the AGNSW to discuss progress on preserving Australia's digital heritage. Knowledge sharing is key.

The fourth challenge is the lack of standardised 'best practice' guidelines on how best to take care of digital artefacts.[5] Prof. Swalwell and Dr Moya are currently working with other cultural institutions in the EaaSI network to develop best practice methods and guidelines so there can be a standard across Australian organisations regarding the preservation and future accessibility of complex digital artefacts. Without the resources of the lab and its team, there is a great risk that many pieces of Australian artwork, software and video games could be lost due to the risks of digital obsolescence that directly affect earlier operating systems like Windows 95 and 98 and outdated technology like floppy disks, CD-ROMS, and old hard drives.

Seeing the labour required to make everything 'work' was a challenge in itself. Prior to my time at the Digital Heritage Lab, I had only read about the theoretical ability to build virtual environments for emulation and compare prior versions of digital artefacts with new copies to manage their preservation. I then had the invaluable opportunity to participate in the full workflow: cleaning a floppy disk, imaging it using Applesauce, and inspecting the information that could have been damaged (bit loss was common); and viewing the image and converting it into a software file to test in emulation. I also helped capture information about the software or game I was imaging which could then be exported into a catalogue for the Australian Computer Museum Society. This kind of 'back end' work in digital preservation was not something I had much knowledge about before coming to the lab. Experiencing the full suite of end-to-end digital preservation through copying and comparing disks reconfirmed aspects of my learning. Taking something that was sitting in someone's garage, cleaning it, and uploading it to EaaSI to allow for the possibility of future research helped me appreciate the idea that access is a key component of understanding information architecture. Preservation does not end with safekeeping – the things preserved also need to be accessible.[6]

Something I did not expect was people's enthusiastic response when they found out about my interest in gaming as a hobby. Growing up, all my friends and family played games, so I assumed that the people I would be working with would also be avid gamers like me (regularly playing games for more than a few hours a week). This was not the case! Game preservation as an extension of media archiving was mostly an intellectual and professional pursuit that focused on preserving Australian game history, whether or not those games were classified as 'good' or 'bad'. I never thought my casual skill as a gamer would help Dr Moya and the lab, but I was able to capture native gameplay footage to compare with the emulation project the lab was undertaking with the EaaSI platform.

Overall though, the most valuable thing I learned was perseverance in the face of failure – a valuable life skill for information professionals. The most difficult task Dr Moya challenged me with during my placement was getting a native Windows 95 computer to stream directly onto a modern laptop for a game-play recording for comparison (native versus emulation). I had 'Frankensteined' together a Video Graphics Array (VGA) splitter, an Open-Source Scan Converter (OSSC), a tangle of HDMI cables and a Capture Card setup for a modern laptop. It was the first time I had ever had to assemble something of that magnitude in any professional context (would there ever be a textbook that describes the process of using a VGA splitter for digital archivists, I wondered). Once I had the cables set up, I then had to get the Windows 95 screen captured using Open Broadcaster Software. The best part of the process was experimenting, testing and then writing everything down to see what did and did not work. I was discouraged when all my solutions failed to get the results I was hoping for, but Dr Moya insisted I keep experimenting. I was able to use her and her knowledge of hardware as a sounding board for my ideas and they were all encouraged. Eventually, after a day and a half of attempts, I got it working and could make the recording we needed. This was an incredible breakthrough, as the lab required recordings to compare native Windows 95 footage to emulated software through EaaSI. I felt like I had made a genuine difference.

The placement with the Digital Heritage Lab was indispensable in my personal development as an information professional. I received hands-on experience with equipment and techniques currently used within GLAM institutions and was able to meet and talk with information professionals like Dr Moya and Prof. Swalwell to discuss where I would like to go in my career. The skills I learned during my short period at the lab led to an employment opportunity with the SLNSW, where I used the skills I acquired imaging CD-ROMS and floppy disks in my day-to-day work, preserving digital objects from the library's collection.

Although the academic knowledge I had gained during my university degree set a solid bedrock of archival theory, it was the practical work of experimenting – and failing – that I found more beneficial in the end. The same could be said for the wider field of digital archiving, where practical testing and experimentation remain central to the pursuit of preserving digital artefacts.

Notes on contributor

Bryony Cavallaro is currently working as a Digital Archives Assistant at the State Library of NSW while finishing her Master of Information Studies at Charles Sturt University. She is passionate about finding long-term solutions to preserving complex digital artefacts, like video games, and contributing to the development of digital preservation practice in Australia.

Notes

1. ML Swalwell, H Stuckey, D De Vries, C Moya, C Cranmer, S Frost, A Goddard, S Miller, C Murphy and N Richardson, 'Archiving Australian Media Arts: A Project Overview', Preservation, Digital Technology & Culture, vol. 51, no. 4, 2022, pp. 155–166.
2. AG Howell, Preserving Digital Information: Challenges and Solutions, Victorian Academic Libraries, Victorian University Libraries and State Library of Victoria, Melbourne, 2004.
3. G Oliver and R Harvey, Digital Curation, Second Edition, American Library Association, 2017.

4. Software Preservation Network, 'Emulation As A Service Infrastructure', 2024, available at https://www.softwarepreservationnetwork.org/emulation-as-a-service-infrastructure/, accessed 14 February 2024.
5. Digital Preservation Coalition, 'Digital Preservation Handbook – Preservation Issues', 2023, available at https://www.dpconline.org/handbook/digital-preservation/preservation-issues, accessed 19 October 2023.
6. Australian Library and Information Association, 'Foundation Knowledge, Skills and Attributes for Information Professionals Working in Archives, Libraries and Records Management', 2020, available at https://www.alia.org.au/common/Uploaded%20files/ALIA-Docs/2021/Foundation_knowledge_skills_and_attributes_relevant_to_information_professionals.pdf, accessed 19 October 2023.

www.ingramcontent.com/pod-product-compliance
Lightning Source LLC
Chambersburg PA
CBHW080402030426
42334CB00024B/2965